VISUAL QUICKSTART GUIDE

HTML

FOR THE WORLD WIDE WEB

Elizabeth Castro

Peachpit Press

Visual QuickStart Guide
HTML for the World Wide Web
Elizabeth Castro

Peachpit Press
2414 Sixth Street
Berkeley, CA 94710
(510) 548-4393
(510) 548-5991 (fax)

Find us on the World Wide Web at: http://www.peachpit.com

Peachpit Press is a division of Addison-Wesley Publishing Company

Copyright © 1996 by Elizabeth Castro
All photographs copyright © 1996 by Elizabeth Castro

Cover design: The Visual Group

ISBN: 0-201-88448-8

0 9 8 7 6 5 4

Printed and bound in the United States of America

♻ Printed on recycled paper

For my parents
(all four of them!)
who didn't always agree,
but who supported me anyway.

Special thanks to:

Nolan Hester at Peachpit for his great suggestions and for his patience when I added new sections at the second to last moment.

Matthew Crocker and *Greg Anderson* at Crocker Communications for their help and technical advice.

Andreu Cabré for his feedback, for his great Photoshop tips, and for sharing his life with me.

Llumi and *Xixo* for chasing cherry tomatoes and each other around my office and for helping me think up examples of HTML documents.

TABLE OF CONTENTS

Table of contents

INTRODUCTION

Why would you want to publish an HTML page? Simply, to communicate with the world. The World Wide Web is the Gutenberg press of our time. Practically anyone can publish any kind of information, including graphics, sound and even video, on the Web, opening the doors to each and every one of the millions of Internet users. Some are businesses with services to sell, others are individuals with stories to share. You decide how your page will be.

HTML is not hard to learn or to master. It is much more an exercise in careful typing and consistency than in mind-blowing, complicated procedures. You can have a simple HTML page up and running in just a few minutes. As your page gets more complicated, you will still find that the design of the elements on the page takes up much more time than writing the actual HTML code.

In this book, you'll find clear, easy-to-follow instructions that will take you through the process step-by-step. It is perfect for the beginner, with no knowledge of HTML, who wants to begin to create HTML pages.

You can also use the book as a reference, looking up topics in the hefty index and consulting just those subjects that you need information on.

All of the examples shown in this book can be found at *http://www.peachpit. com/peachpit/features/htmlvqs/ htmlvqs.html.* See you on the Web.

HTML and the Web

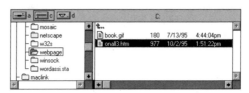

Somehow, it shouldn't be surprising that the lingua franca of the World Wide Web was developed in Switzerland, which has four official state languages. Perhaps acutely aware of how difficult it is for people to communicate without a common language, the programmers at the CERN research lab created a kind of Esperanto for computers: the Hypertext Markup Language, or HTML.

Figure i-1. *It doesn't matter if the original file is from a Windows machine (above), a Macintosh (right) or any other computer, as long as it uses HTML coding and is saved as a text-only file.*

onallthree.html

HTML allows you to format text, add rules, graphics, sound, and video and save it all in a text-only ASCII file that any computer can read. (Of course, to project video or play sounds, the computer must have the necessary hardware.) The key to HTML is in the *tags*, keywords enclosed in less than (<) and greater than (>) signs, that indicate what kind of content is coming up.

Of course, HTML just looks like a lot of text sprinkled with greater than and less than signs until you open the file with a special program called a *browser*. A browser can interpret the HTML tags and then show the formatted document on screen.

Figure i-2. *Each computer (Unix, top left), Windows, above and Mac, left) shows the HTML code in its own way. The results are actually very similar; the differences are mostly cosmetic.*

HTML is not just another way to create beautiful documents, however. Its key ingredient is in the first part of its name: *Hypertext.* HTML documents can contain links to other HTML documents or to practically anything else on the Internet. This means that you can create several Web pages and have your users jump from one to another as needed. You can also create links to other organizations' Web pages, giving your users access to information held at other sites.

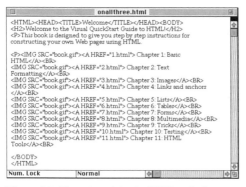

Figure i-3. *There is nothing in HTML code that cannot be expressed with simple numbers, letters and symbols. This makes it easy for any kind of computer system to understand it.*

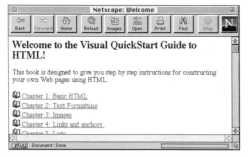

Figure i-4. *This is a browser on the Macintosh. Notice the graphic icons and different font sizes.*

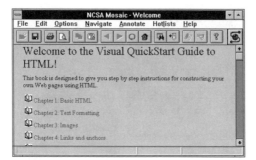

Figure i-5. *This is a browser in Windows showing the same HTML document. The differences are pretty minor.*

Users vs. Programmers

Think for a minute about the wide variety of computers that exist in the world. Each and every one of them can read HTML, but they all do it in a slightly different way—according to what is allowed in their particular operating system. For example, some computers can only display text: letters and numbers, a few symbols, but no graphics or color of any kind.

On the other hand, Windows and Macintosh systems were practically created with graphics and color in mind. Even so, Windows machines tend to be limited to displaying 256 colors while Macintoshes generally are not.

In addition, the way that your users will connect to the Internet may affect the way their computer can view Web pages. Even a Mac user won't be able to see the graphics on your pages if he or she is connected to the Web through a Unix shell account, or through telnet.

Further, there is a big difference between the user who connects to the Web with a slow computer, through a slow modem, and the user who has a direct, high speed connection, and a computer that can make the most of it. The first user will go crazy waiting for images to download while the second may not even notice a delay.

Finally, many browsers let the user decide how to view certain elements on a Web page. The user might be able to change the text and background colors, the text formatting, or even whether or not to show graphics.

Therefore, it is important to realize that each person who looks at your page may see it in a different way, according to the kind of computer system they have, the browser they have chosen, the graphics capacity they have, the speed of their modem and connection to the Web and the settings they have chosen for their browser.

You, as the programmer or designer of the Web page, have *limited control* over how the page actually looks once it reaches your user, the person who is seeing your page through a browser. The primary concern of HTML is that your page be understandable by any computer, not that it be beautiful.

Many people are not satisfied with this lack of control. They add special effects to their pages with nonstandard HTML that may make the pages illegible to many browsers. Or they don't use alternative text for images, thereby restricting meaningful access to their pages to computers with graphics cards and fast Internet connections.

This one is your call. You decide how universal you want your document to be. On the continuum between plain Web pages that can be read by all and beautiful Web masterpieces that can be viewed by just a few, *you* must decide where your pages will fall.

In this book, I refer to the person who designs Web pages as *you* (or sometimes the programmer or designer). On the other hand, the *user* is the person who will look at your Web pages once you've published them.

Figure i-6. *The WIDTH, CENTER and SIZE attributes for the HR tag are Netscape extensions and are not understood by many browsers.*

Figure i-7. *In Netscape, the added attributes make a pattern out of the lines.*

Figure i-8. *In Mosaic, the lines look rather strange.*

Figure i-9. *In Lynx, the lines just take up space.*

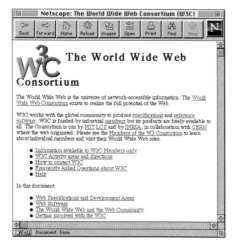

Figure i-10. *The W3 Consortium home page adheres to standard HTML 2 code, which means that this attractive, well-organized page can be viewed with almost any browser.*

Figure i-11. *This page uses several non-standard HTML tags (although less than you might think). There is a white background, and the bottom half of the page is laid out in a table. That means that this striking page will not be as striking unless the user views it with Netscape.*

Different versions of HTML

Democracy can be a great thing: many people give their input and a consensus is reached that aims to satisfy the largest group of people. The Internet is democracy in action. While the original HTML standard was developed by CERN, new versions are hashed out through a series of online meetings open to anyone on the Internet. Then they are analyzed, discussed, decided and published by the W3 Consortium, led by the Laboratory for Computer Science at the Massachusetts Institute of Technology (MIT) and INRIA, a French technology group, in collaboration with CERN.

There is one annoying thing about democracy: it's incredibly slow. At press time, although HTML 2 is considered the current standard, the actual guidelines had not yet been finalized. Nevertheless, HTML 3 is on the way—purportedly by the end of 1995, with many of the new features already incorporated into some browsers.

Take a look at the two main groups who are discussing and deciding the future of HTML. On the one hand there is the W3 Consortium, careful to request input from as many sides as possible and to create a version of HTML that is, first and foremost, universal and that is as rich as universality allows. On the other side of the fence are the commercial interests, like Netscape Communications, that are anxious to add features to HTML in order to gain users—even if the resulting HTML cannot be read by every single computer system or user.

Different versions of HTML

Different versions of HTML

Netscape Communications, for example, frustrated with the lengthy discussions, went ahead and created a series of *extensions* to HTML that only Netscape's browser, Netscape Navigator (often referred to as simply Netscape), can read.

Netscape's extensions give more power to the programmer and take it away from the user. They let you add formatting, center text and graphics, align graphics, choose bullet shape in lists and many others. However, if your user views your page with a browser that does not support Netscape's extensions, he or she will not see the added formatting, although in most cases, he or she will see the page—in a stripped down form.

Nevertheless, the popularity of Netscape's extensions have made Netscape Navigator the most popular browser for the World Wide Web, used by some 70% of the population. All of these factors are helping to get the HTML discussion rolling at a faster pace. If the folks at W3 Consortium want to keep HTML universal, they will have to move faster at incorporating new standards into the HTML language.

In this book, you will learn both standard HTML as well as the Netscape extensions that have become so popular. Netscape extensions are marked with the Netscape Only icon **(Figure i-12)**.

Figure i-12. *If the entire technique is "Netscape Only", the icon appears in the introduction. If only one part of the technique is Netscape specific, the icon appears in that particular step.*

HTML browsers

Perhaps the most important tool for creating HTML documents is the HTML browser. You might think that only your users need to have a browser, but you'd be wrong. It is absolutely vital that you have at least one, and preferably three or four of the principal browsers in use around the world. This way you can test your HTML pages and make sure that they look the way you want them to—regardless of the browser used.

Netscape Navigator

According to the latest statistics floating around the Net, Netscape Navigator (most often referred to simply as *Netscape*) is used by over 70% of the Web browsing public. Developed by some of the same engineers who created Mosaic (see next page), Netscape has distanced itself from the competition by offering non-standard features that make Netscape enhanced pages much more attractive to the eye—if much more taxing to the modem.

Besides the complete set of HTML 2, Netscape supports HTML 3's tables in addition to what are commonly called the *Netscape extensions*: cosmetic additions that you can add to your pages and that only Netscape currently knows how to interpret. With Netscape's extensions, you can add new background, text and link colors, change the bullets and numbering scheme in lists, use special alignment options and many others.

Netscape Navigator is available for Macintosh and Windows. Although you can download a copy for review for 30 days, if you decide to keep it, it costs $50. Netscape Communications is quite particular about only giving support to registered users.

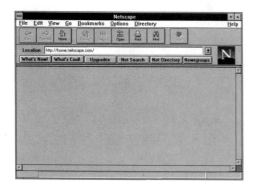

Figure i-13. *Netscape Navigator is the most popular browser for Macintosh and Windows, used by some 70% of the population. This is Macintosh version 2.0.*

Figure i-14. *The Windows version of Netscape Navigator is virtually identical to the Mac version, although the window itself acts differently, adding or hiding navigation buttons as it gets bigger or smaller.*

NCSA Mosaic

NCSA Mosaic holds the tenuous second place position in the Browser Olympics, although its influence is disappearing quickly, thanks to Netscape's dominance and the Internet browser from Microsoft included with Windows 95.

Mosaic was the most popular browser during the beginning part of the Web's popularity explosion, and was developed by the National Center for Supercomputing Applications (NCSA) at the University of Illinois. Mosaic is available for Macintosh **(Figure i-15)**, Windows **(Figure i-16)** and others. It is distributed free of charge.

Lynx

Lynx is the most widely used text-only browser. Users with only a dial-up connection to a Unix account (like many university students) use Lynx to access the Web. It is fast and efficient. Although pages may look more attractive in Netscape and Mosaic, they appear faster with Lynx **(Figure i-17)**.

Lynx supports HTML 2, including forms, but not tables. Inline graphics are not displayed; the alternative text shows in its place. There is a DOS version of Lynx that can be combined with helper applications to show images.

Figure i-15. *NCSA Mosaic is a perfectly, good browser, if slighlty more rudimentary than Netscape. Future versions are promised that recognize many of the Netscape extensions. This is version 2 for Mac.*

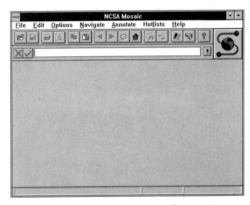

Figure i-16. *The Windows version of NCSA Mosaic is very similar to the Macintosh version.*

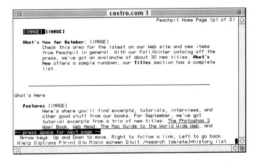

Figure i-17. *Lynx is the most common browser for Unix systems.*

Writing HTML

You can create an HTML document with any word processor or text editor, including the very basic TeachText or SimpleText on the Mac and Write for Windows, both of which come free with the corresponding system software.

Nevertheless, there are certain tools that may help you create HTML documents. These are discussed on pages 147-156.

HTML Tags

HTML tags are commands written between less than (<) and greater than (>) signs, also known as *angle brackets*, that indicate how the browser should display the text. There are opening and closing versions for many tags, and the affected text is *contained* within the two tags. Both the opening and closing tags use the same command word but the closing tag carries an initial extra forward slash symbol /.

Figure 1-1. *The anatomy of an HTML tag. Notice there are no extra spaces between the contained text and the angle brackets (greater than and less than signs).*

Attributes

Many tags have special attributes that offer a variety of options for the contained text. The attribute is entered between the command word and the final greater than symbol. Often, you can use a series of attributes in a single tag. Simply write one after the other, with a space between each·one.

Figure 1-2. *Some tags can take optional* attributes *that further define the formatting desired.*

Values

Attributes in turn often have *values*. In some cases, you must pick a value from a small group of choices. For example, the CLEAR attribute for the BR tag can take values of *left, right* and *all*. Any other value given will be ignored.

Other attributes are more strict about the *type* of values they accept. For example, the HSPACE attribute of the IMG tag will accept only integers as its value, and the SRC attribute of the IMG tag will only accept URLs for its value.

Quotation marks

Generally speaking, attributes that accept any value require that you enclose the value in straight quotation marks (") NOT curly ones (""). It is a good idea to use quotes around any URL to ensure that any extra spaces and punctuation are not misinterpreted by the server.

Nesting tags

In some cases, you may want to modify your page contents with more than one tag. For example, you may want to add italic formatting to a word inside a header. There are two things to keep in mind here. First, not all tags can contain all other kinds of tags. In this book, each tag's description details which other tags it may contain and which tags it may not.

Second, order is everything. Whenever you use a closing tag it should correspond to the last unclosed opening tag. In other words, first A then B, then /B, and then /A **(Figure 1-5)**.

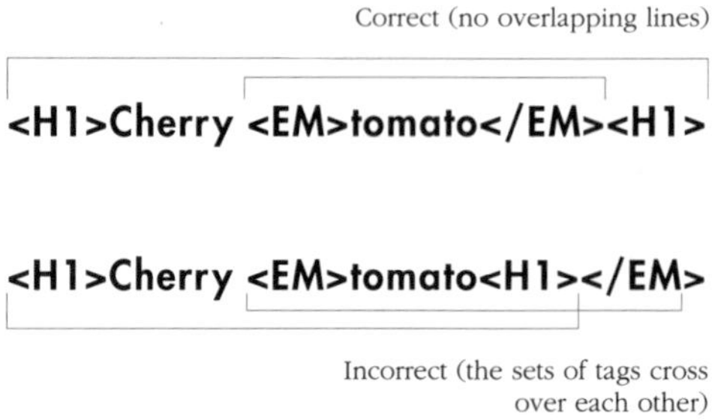

Value for CLEAR

<BR CLEAR=left>

Figure 1-3. *Some tags, like BR shown here, take attributes with given* values, *of which you can choose only one. You don't need to enclose one word values in quotation marks.*

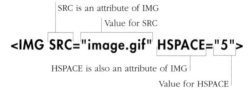

SRC is an attribute of IMG

Value for SRC

<IMG SRC="image.gif" HSPACE="5">

HSPACE is also an attribute of IMG

Value for HSPACE

Figure 1-4. *Some tags, like IMG shown here, can take more than one attribute, each with its own values.*

Correct (no overlapping lines)

<H1>Cherry <EM>tomato</EM><H1>

<H1>Cherry <EM>tomato<H1></EM>

Incorrect (the sets of tags cross over each other)

Figure 1-5: *To make sure your tags are correctly nested, connect each set with a line. None of your sets of tags should overlap any other set; each interior set should be completely enclosed within the larger set.*

Protocol Server name (domain) Path

<http://www.site.com/liz/file.html>

File name

Figure 1-6. *Your basic URL contains a protocol, server name, path and file name.*

Trailing forward slash

<http://www.site.com/liz/>

Figure 1-7. *A URL with a trailing forward slash and no file name points to the default file in the last directory named (in this case the* liz *directory). The default file on many servers is* index.html.

Protocol Server name Path

<ftp://ftp.site.com/pub/prog.exe>

File name

Figure 1-8. *When the user clicks this URL, the browser will begin an FTP transfer of the file* prog.exe.

Protocol Path

<http://cookie/baby.html>

File name

Figure 1-9. *A relative URL contains the protocol and an abbreviated path followed by the file name. If this URL was in the HTML file at the following location:* www.site.com/WWW/liz/file.html, *the above URL would be interpreted as* http://www.site.com/ WWW/liz/cookie/baby.html.

Protocol Path

<http://../andreu/go/index.html>

File name

Figure 1-10. *If this URL was found within the file at* www.site.com/WWW/liz/file.html, *the full URL would be interpreted as* http://www.site.com/ WWW/andreu/go/index.html.

URLs

A uniform resource locator, or URL, is a fancy name for an address. It contains information about where a file is and what a browser should do with it. Each file has a unique URL.

The first part of the URL is called the *protocol*. It tells the browser how to deal with the file that it is about to open. One of the most common protocols you will see is HTTP, or Hypertext Transfer Protocol. It is used to access Web pages. The protocol is generally followed by two forward slashes (two major exceptions are the mailto and news protocols).

The second part of the URL is the name of the server where the file is located, followed by the path that leads to the file and the file's name itself. Sometimes, a URL ends in a trailing forward slash with no file name given. In this case the URL refers to the default file in the last directory in the path (which generally corresponds to the home page).

URLs can be either absolute or relative. An absolute URL shows the entire path to the file. A relative URL gives only the protocol and a part of the path. The browser constructs the rest of the path according to the current location of the file that contains the URL. Directories inside the current directory are indicated with a forward slash (/). Directories above the current file in the server's hierarchy are noted with two periods (..).

Generally, you should always use relative URLs. They make it easy to move your pages from a local system to a server—as long as the relative position of each file remains constant, the links are not lost. Use absolute URLs when linking to pages on remote servers.

Special symbols

The standard ASCII set contains 128 characters and can be used perfectly well for English documents. However, accents, diacritical marks and many commonly used symbols unfortunately cannot be found in this group. Luckily, HTML can contain any character in the full ISO Latin-1 character set (also known as ISO 8859-1). In Windows and Unix systems, simply enter the character in the usual (convoluted) way and it will display properly in the browser.

Watch out! Even though you can type special characters, accents and so on in your Macintosh and DOS based PC, these systems do not use the standard ISO Latin-1 character set for the characters numbered 129-255, and will not display them correctly in the Web page. You must enter these special characters with either *name* or *number codes.*

Name codes are more descriptive (and are case sensitive), like è for é and Ñ for Ñ. However, not every character has a name code. In that case, you will need to use a number code, which is composed of an ampersand, number symbol, the character number in the Latin-1 character set and a semicolon. The number code for é is é and for Ñ is Ñ. See Appendix A for a complete listing and more instructions.

There are four symbols that have special meanings in HTML documents. These are the greater than (>), less than (<), double quotation marks (") and ampersand (&). If you simply type them in your HTML document, the browser may attempt to interpret them **(Figure 1-12)**. To show the symbols themselves, use a name or number code.

Typing a ç on a Mac gets you a Ÿ. (In DOS you'd get a ‡.)

`<H1>Visca el Barça</H1>`

Visca el BarŸa

The number code for ç.

`<H1>Visca el Bar&#231;a</H1>`

Visca el Barça

In the Web page

Figure 1-11. *To display a ç properly, you must use either its number or its name. It looks awful in your HTML document, but on the Web page, where it counts, it's beautiful.*

If you type < and >...

Use `<BR>` for line breaks

...the BR tag is interpreted and creates a line break

Use
for line breaks

If you use name codes for < and >...

Use `&lt;BR&gt;` for line breaks

the symbols are shown but not interpreted

Use `<BR>` for line breaks

Figure 1-12. *You must use name or number codes to show the symbols <, >, ", and & on your Web page. See Appendix A for more details.*

Extra returns

Figure 1-13. *Extra returns and spaces help distinguish the different parts of the HTML document in the text editor but are completely ignored by the browser.*

Paragraph tag

Figure 1-14. *I've removed all the returns from the document in Figure 1-13, but added a single <P> tag. The only difference in the final result is from the new tag.*

Spacing

HTML browsers will ignore any extra spaces that exist between the tags in your HTML document. You can use this to your advantage by adding spaces and returns to help view the elements in your HTML document more clearly while you're writing and designing your page **(Figure 1-13)**.

On the other hand, you won't be able to count on returns or spaces to format your document. A return at the end of a paragraph in your HTML document will not appear in the browsed page. Instead, use a P tag to begin each new paragraph **(Figure 1-14)**.

Finally, you cannot repeat several P (or BR) tags to add space between paragraphs. The extra tags are simply ignored.

Tags with automatic line breaks

Some tags include automatic, logical line breaks. For example, you don't need to use a new paragraph marker after a header, since a header automatically includes a line break **(Figure 1-14)**. In fact, inserting a new paragraph marker after a header has no effect whatsoever.

Starting and finishing an HTML document

When a user jumps to the URL that corresponds to your Web page, the browser needs information right away about what kind of document it is, and how it should be displayed. It gets this information from the HTML tag, which also identifies your document so that it can be recognized by other applications across the Internet, including WAIS databases and other indexing and searching systems.

Figure 1-15. *The HTML tag identifies your document so that the browser knows how to display it.*

To start and finish an HTML document:

1. Type **<HTML>**.

2. Create your HTML document.

3. Type **</HTML>**.

✔ Tips

■ Yes, it is true that most browsers will still recognize your document and display it correctly even if you don't use the HTML tag. However, standard HTML requires that the tag be used. As the Web becomes more complicated and more types of documents can be accessed by a browser, the HTML tag will become increasingly more important to identify your file as an HTML page.

■ Create an HTML document template (with the opening and closing HTML tags already typed in) as a starting place for all your HTML documents.

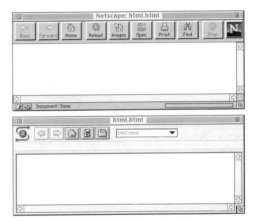

Figure 1-16. *An empty HTML document will appear empty in the browser as well (Netscape top, Mosaic bottom), with the file name as title.*

Figure 1-17. *Every HTML document should be divided into a HEAD and a BODY.*

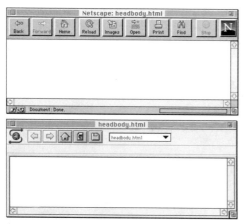

Figure 1-18. *With no title and no contents, this browser has to scrape together a little substance (in the form of a title) from the file name of the HTML document.*

The HEAD and BODY

The HEAD section provides information about the URL of your Web page as well as its relationship with the other pages at your site. The only element in the HEAD section that is visible to the user is the title of the Web page (see page 8).

To create the HEAD section:

1. Directly after the initial HTML tag (<HTML>), type **<HEAD>**.

2. Create the HEAD section, including the TITLE (page 8) and the BASE (page 62), if desired.

3. Type **</HEAD>**.

The BODY of your HTML document contains the bulk of your Web page, including all the text, graphics and formatting.

To create the BODY:

1. After the final </HEAD> tag and before anything else, type **<BODY>**.

2. Create the contents of your Web page.

3. Type **</BODY>**. The only element permitted after the final BODY tag is the final HTML tag (</HTML>).

The HEAD and BODY

Creating a title

Each HTML page must have a title. A title should be short and descriptive. In some browsers, the title appears in the title bar of the window; in others, the title is centered at the top of the screen. The title is used in indexes as well as in browsers' history lists and bookmarks.

Figure 1-19. *The TITLE tag is the only element in the HEAD section that is visible to the user.*

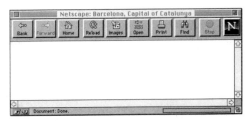

Figure 1-20. *Netscape shows the title of a Web page in the title bar of the window.*

Figure 1-21. *Mosaic shows the title of a Web page in the title bar, as well as in the History pop-up menu at the top of the window.*

To create a title:

1. Place the cursor between the opening and closing HEAD tags.

2. Type **<TITLE>**.

3. Enter the title of your web page.

4. Type **</TITLE>**.

✔ Tips

■ A title cannot contain any formatting, images, or links to other pages.

■ Don't use colons or backslashes in your titles. These symbols cannot be used by some operating systems for file names, and if someone tries to save your page as text (or source HTML), they will have to remove the offending character manually.

■ Use a common element to begin each page's title. For example, you could begin each page with "XYZ Company -" followed by the specific area described on that page.

■ If your title has special characters like accents or foreign letters, you'll have to format these characters with their character or entity references. (See Appendix A.)

■ For animated titles, see page 127.

Figure 1-22. *Don't repeat the information from your title in your header. The header should help organize the information on the page in sections while the title summarizes that information.*

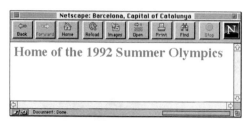

Figure 1-23. *Try to keep your header text to one line or less. Otherwise, you will fill up the user's screen before they get to your text.*

Figure 1-24. *Mosaic shows level 1 headers at a smaller size than Netscape.*

Organizing the page

HTML provides for up to six levels of headers in your Web page. You will seldom have to use more than three. Since headers can be used to compile a table of contents of your Web pages, you should be as consistent as possible when applying them.

To use headers to organize your Web page:

1. In the BODY section of your HTML document, type **<Hn>**, where *n* is a number from 1 to 6, depending on the level of header that you want to create.

2. Type the contents of the header.

3. Type **</Hn>** where *n* is the same number used in step 1.

✔ Tips

- Think of your headers as chapter names—they are hierarchical dividers. Use them consistently.

- Headers are formatted logically: the higher the level (the smaller the number), the more prominently the header will be displayed. The actual formatting used may differ from browser to browser.

- Add a named anchor to your headers so that you can create links directly to that header from a different web page. (See pages 64-65.)

- Headers have an automatic line break; there is no need (nor gain) to add an additional one.

Starting a new paragraph

HTML does not recognize the returns that you enter in your text editor. To start a new paragraph in your Web page, you must use the P tag.

To begin a new paragraph:

1. Type **<P>**.

2. Type the contents of the new paragraph.

3. If desired, you may type **</P>** to end the paragraph, but it is not necessary.

✔ Tip

■ The header (Hn) and horizontal rule (HR) tags include automatic paragraph markers, so you don't need to add a <P> to start a new paragraph after using them **(Figure 1-25)**.

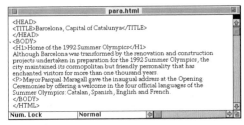

Figure 1-25. *Since headers include automatic line breaks, there is no need to include a <P> before the first paragraph. You do need to insert a <P> before the second paragraph.*

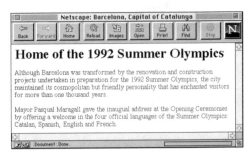

Figure 1-26 (Netscape). *Unfortunately, there is presently no way to precisely control the amount of spacing between paragraphs with the <P> tag.*

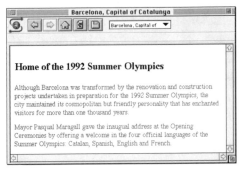

Figure 1-27 (Mosaic). *Notice how the divisions from line to line are different from browser to browser. It is important to realize just what you can and cannot control.*

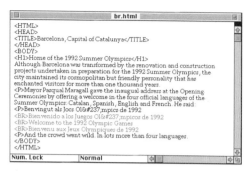

Figure 1-28. *I've used a P tag to start the first line to set the group off from the remaining text. Then, each "welcome" is separated with a line break.*

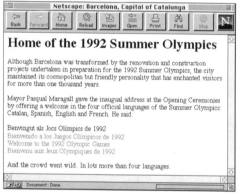

Figure 1-29. *I have to admit, I don't actually remember what Maragall said in French. Perhaps he was drowned out by the crowd and I didn't hear him...*

Figure 1-30. *Mosaic uses slightly different formatting, but the weight given each tag is consistent.*

Creating a line break

When you start a new paragraph with the P tag (described on the previous page), most browsers insert a large amount of space. To begin a new line without so much space, use a line break.

The BR tag is perfect for poems or other short lines of text that should appear one after another without a lot of space in between.

To insert a line break:

1. Type **
** where the line break should occur. There is no closing BR tag.

✔ Tip

■ Netscape has created special extensions for using line breaks with text that is wrapped around images. See page 51 for details.

Creating a line break

Adding comments to your pages

One diagnostic tool available to every HTML author is the addition of comments to your HTML documents to remind you (or future editors) what you were trying to achieve with your HTML tags.

These comments appear only in the HTML document when opened with a text or HTML editor. They will be completely invisible to the user.

To add comments to your HTML page:

1. In your HTML document, where you wish to insert comments, type **<!--**.

2. Type the comments. Comments are particularly useful for describing why you used a particular tag and what effect you were hoping to achieve.

3. Type **-->** to complete the commented text.

✔ Tips

■ Another good use for comments is to remind yourself (or future editors) to include, remove or update certain sections.

■ View your commented page with a browser before publishing (see Chapter 10) to avoid sharing your (possibly) private comments with your public.

■ Beware, however, of comments that are *too* private. While invisible in the browser, they cheerfully reappear when the user saves the page as HTML code (source).

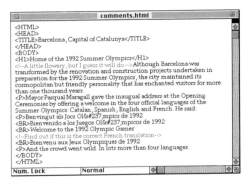

Figure 1-31. *Comments are a great way to add reminders to your text. You can also use them to keep track of revisions and sections that need to be revised.*

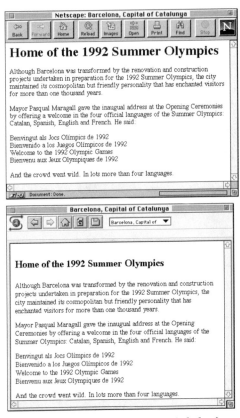

Figure 1-32 (Netscape above, Mosaic below). *The comments are completely invisible to the user— unless he or she downloads the source HTML.*

TEXT FORMATTING

One of the special things about the Web is that you can format your pages in a *logical* way—indicating which paragraphs or words are important rather than assigning specific fonts and sizes. Each individual browser then uses the formatting capabilities of the local computer to give emphasis in its own way.

In this chapter, you'll learn how to use both logical and physical formatting tags.

Emphasizing text logically

HTML provides two ways to emphasize your text: with logical markers that identify your text as "emphatic" or "strong" and with physical markers that identify the text as "bold" or "italic". Logical markers allow your *users* to choose how to view important text—perhaps in bold red lettering—throughout all their web pages, while physical formatting appears how you, the page's *designer* intended, as long as the browser supports your formatting choices.

To emphasize text logically:

1. Type **<EM>** or **<STRONG>**. Text formatted with EM generally appears in italics. Text formatted with STRONG most often appears in bold. In some browsers, the user can change the display of either of these two formats.

2. Type the emphatic or strong text.

3. Type **</EM>** or **</STRONG>**.

✔ Tips

■ Logical formatting ensures that the text will receive some formatting in the event that the browser does not recognize certain types of physical formatting.

■ Don't emphasize everything. If you shout everything at your viewers, you will lose their confidence and their attention.

■ You may not add emphasis to titles or form elements. In some browsers, block quotes can include the EM tag but not the STRONG tag.

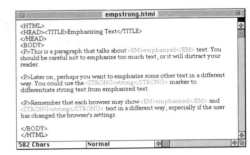

Figure 2-1. *Creating emphatic or strong text on your web page is as simple as adding the appropriate marker before and after the text to be formatted.*

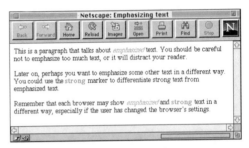

Figure 2-2. *Netscape displays emphatic text in italics and strong text in bold.*

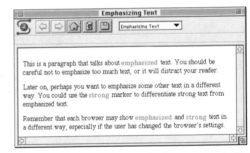

Figure 2-3. *NCSA Mosaic's default settings use bold formatting for both emphatic and strong text. Your users may change the settings to display emphatic text in italics (or any other way they choose).*

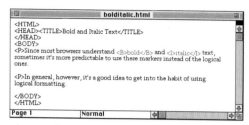

Figure 2-4. *You may use bold or italic formatting anywhere in your HTML document, except in the TITLE.*

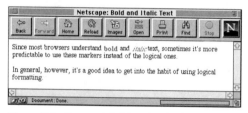

Figure 2-5. *Netscape's bold and italic formatting are identical to its strong and emphatic formatting, respectively.*

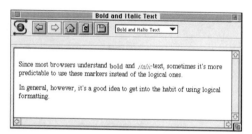

Figure 2-6. *NCSA Mosaic shows bold and italic formatting as you might expect.*

Making text bold or italic

There are several physical markers you can use to make your text stand out. In general, you should use logical formatting (EM and STRONG) for making text bold and italic, respectively. (See previous page.) Use physical formatting when you don't want the user to be able to change the display of the text.

To make text bold:

1. Type **<B>**.

2. Type the text that you want to make bold.

3. Type **</B>**.

To make text italic:

1. Type **<I>**.

2. Type the text that you want to make italic.

3. Type **</I>**.

✔ Tips

■ Remember that not all browsers can display text in bold and italics. If they do not recognize the tags, the text will have no formatting at all.

■ You may use CITE (the citation marker) to make text italic, although it is less widely recognized and less widely used than the I marker.

Making text bold or italic

Using a monospaced font

If you are displaying computer codes, URLs or other text that you wish to offset from the main page, you can format it with a monospaced font. There are several markers that use a monospaced font as their principal attribute: CODE (computer code), KBD (keyboard input), SAMP (sample text) and TT (typewriter text), only the last of which is considered physical formatting.

To format text with a monospaced font:

1. Type **<CODE>**, **<KBD>**, **<SAMP>** or **<TT>**.

2. Type the text that you want to display in a monospaced font.

3. Type **</CODE>**, **</KBD>**, **</SAMP>** or **</TT>**. Use the marker that matches the code you chose in step 1.

✔ Tips

■ TT is the monospaced font marker that is used most often.

■ Remember that the monospaced font markers will not have a very dramatic effect in browsers that display all their text in monospaced fonts (like Lynx).

■ To format several lines of monospaced text, you should use the PRE marker. (See page 21.)

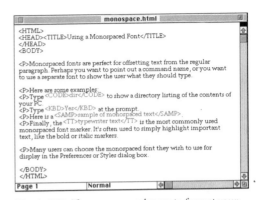

Figure 2-7. *There are several ways to format your text with a monospaced font. TT is the most common.*

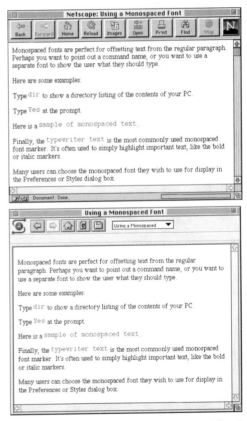

Figure 2-8. *Both Netscape (top) and Mosaic (above) display each of the monospaced font examples identically: with the same size and font as was chosen in the Preferences dialog box.*

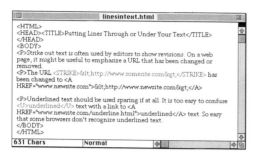

Figure 2-9. *Note the use of < and > to produce the less than and greater than symbols as shown below. (See page 4 and Appendix A.)*

Strike out text works nicely in this HTML document. In Netscape (below), it is understood and helps the user. In NCSA Mosaic (bottom) it is ignored, but doesn't confuse the user.

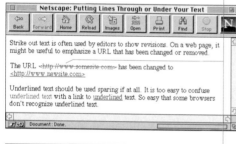

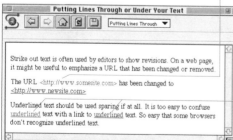

Figure 2-10. *Here is a perfect example to demonstrate the limitations you face as a programmer. Both browsers show the same HTML document (**Figure 2-9**), but the first understands underlining but not strike outs and the second understands strike outs but not underlining. You can't control which browser your users will use.*

Striking out or underlining text

A few browsers can display lines either through or under text. Strike out text is most useful to show revisions to text. Underlining is another way of emphasizing text.

To strike out or underline text:

1. Type **<STRIKE>** or **<U>** for strike out text and underlining, respectively.

2. Type the text that should appear with a line through or under it.

3. Type **</STRIKE>** or **<U>**.

✔ Tips

- Many browsers don't understand the STRIKE or U tags and will display the strike out or underlined text with no formatting at all.

- Users with black and white or grayscale screens often use underlining to indicate links to other web pages. You may confuse them by underlining text that does not bring them to a new page.

- Lynx displays EM and STRONG text with an underline. Users may be confused by further underlining.

Notice how ambiguous the underlined text appears. It's hard to tell which word is the link, and which is simply underlined.

Striking out or underlining text

Using superscripts and subscripts

Letters or numbers that are raised or lowered slightly relative to the main body text are called superscripts and subscripts, respectively. HTML 3 includes tags for defining both kinds of offset text. Mosaic 2 already recognizes these tags as does Netscape 2.

To create superscripts or subscripts:

1. Type **<SUB>** to create a subscript or **<SUP>** to create a superscript.

2. Type the characters or symbols that you wish to offset relative to the main text.

3. Type **</SUB>** or **</SUP>** according to what you used in step 1 to complete the offset text.

Figure 2-11. *The opening SUP or SUB tag precedes the text to be affected.*

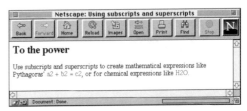

Figure 2-12. *Netscape 1.1 does not recognize the SUB and SUP tags.*

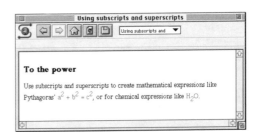

Figure 2-13. *Mosaic displays both subscripts and superscripts correctly.*

Figure 2-14. *Note the different methods used to center headers and to center regular text.*

Figure 2-15. *Netscape centers both headers and regular text correctly. Note that the last paragraph is not centered.*

Figure 2-16. *Mosaic is also capable of centering both headers and regular text correctly.*

Centering text

There are two ways to center text, depending on the kind of text you want to center.

To center headers:

1. Type **<Hn** where *n* is the number that represents the level of the header.

2. Type **ALIGN=center**.

3. Type **>** to complete the header.

4. Type the header text.

5. Type **</Hn>** where *n* is the same number used in step 1.

To center regular text:

1. Type **<CENTER>**.

2. Type the text to be centered.

3. Type **</CENTER>**.

Centering text

Using block quotes

You can use block quotes to set off a section of your text—like a quotation by a famous author—from the surrounding text. As usual, different browsers display block quotes in different ways. Some center the text in an indented paragraph in the middle of the page, while others simply italicize the special text.

To create a block quote:

1. Type **<BLOCKQUOTE>**.

2. Type the desired HTML formatting for the text, like **<P>**, for example.

3. Type the text that you wish to appear set off from the preceding and following text.

4. Complete the HTML tag begun in step 2, if necessary.

5. Type **</BLOCKQUOTE>**.

✔ Tips

■ Text should not be placed directly between the opening and closing BLOCKQUOTE tags, but rather between other HTML tags within the BLOCKQUOTE tags. (However, many browsers will display a block quote correctly even if you ignore this rule.)

■ Block quotes can contain additional text formatting like STRONG or EM.

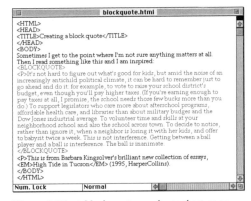

Figure 2-17. *A block quote can be as short or as long as you need. You can even divide it into various paragraphs by adding P tags where necessary.*

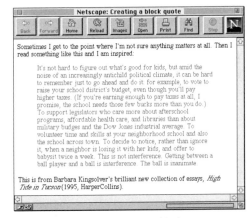

Figure 2-18. *Netscape centers a block quote, indenting it to set it off from the surrounding text.*

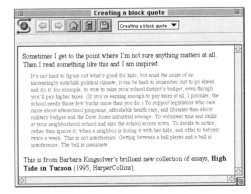

Figure 2-19. *In Mosaic the block quote text is one size smaller than the surrounding text.*

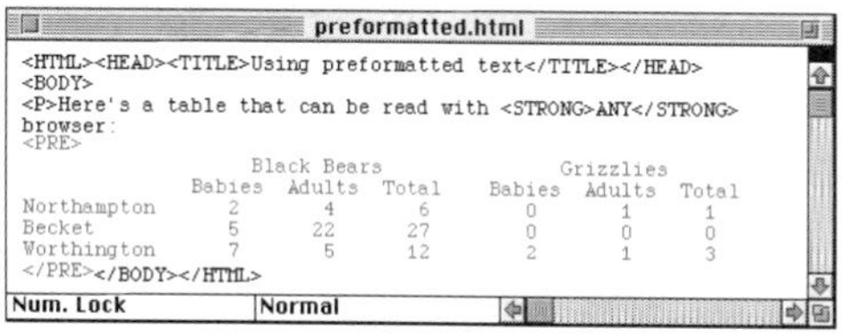

Using preformatted text

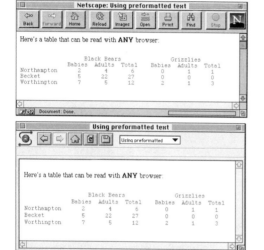

Figure 2-20. *By using a monospaced font, you can see exactly how the preformatted text will appear.*

Figure 2-21. *Both Netscape (above two) and Mosaic (directly above) show preformatted text with a monospaced font.*

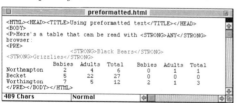

Figure 2-22. *Make sure you don't format the spaces in preformatted text. A bold space takes up more room than a regular one and may throw off your alignment.*

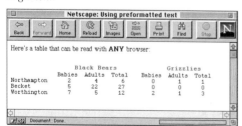

Figure 2-23. *Although the headers looked badly aligned in the HTML document, they look fine in the browser when the tags disappear.*

Usually, each browser decides where to divide each line of text, depending mostly on the window size, and eliminates extra spaces and returns. Preformatted text lets you maintain the original line breaks and spacing that you've inserted in the text. It is ideal for homemade tables and ASCII art.

To use preformatted text:

1. Type **<PRE>**.

2. Type the text that you wish to preformat, with all the necessary spaces, returns and line breaks.

3. Type **</PRE>**.

✔ Tips

■ Since preformatted text is always displayed in a monospaced font (like Courier) by browsers, you should use a monospaced font in your text or HTML editor when composing the text so that you can see what it will look like.

■ You can insert additional formatting (like STRONG or EM) within preformatted text **(Figures 2-22 and 2-23)**. However, you should do it *after* you set up your text, since the tags take up space in the HTML document, but not in the page.

■ You can make homemade tables with preformatted text just by controlling the spaces between column entries. These tables will be readable by *all* browsers, not just the ones that currently support official tables.

■ Use PRE to format an image's alternative text. (See pages 130-131.)

Using preformatted text

Changing the font size

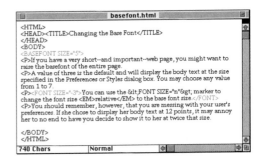

In order to keep HTML documents as universal as possible, the HTML specifications do not let you specify a particular font. The idea is that any user should be able to read your HTML documents, without having to install special fonts in their system. You can, however, choose the relative *size* of the font in order to emphasize certain sections or add a little spice to your page. Netscape uses the BASEFONT and SIZE tags, described on this page. Standard HTML, and thus Mosaic, use the BIG and SMALL tags, described on page 24.

Figure 2-24. *Don't choose a base font size that is too large to fit comfortably in your users' screens.*

To change the font size of the whole page:

1. Type **<BASEFONT**.

2. Type **SIZE="n">** where *n* is a number from 1 to 7. The default is 3, which displays the font at the size the user has chosen in the Preferences or Styles dialog box.

✔ Tips

■ Use a slightly larger basefont in short web pages to give more importance to the whole page. Use a smaller basefont in lengthy text-intensive pages to fit more text on a page.

■ You should use only one BASEFONT marker in each HTML document. The marker will affect all the text after the marker. To change the font size of any additional text, use the FONT marker. (See next page.)

■ To make your font size changes recognizable when viewed by both Netscape and Mosaic, use both kinds of tags at once. (See page 24.)

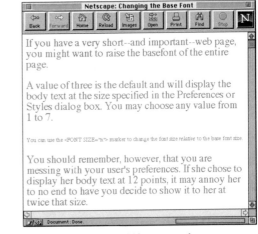

Figure 2-25. *You should have a good reason to change the base font size. Remember that your users have probably already chosen how they prefer to view text.*

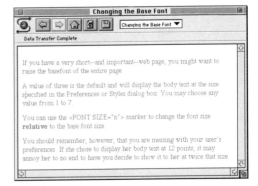

Figure 2-26. *Most browsers, including NCSA Mosaic shown here do not support BASEFONT. (Mosaic does support the BIG and SMALL tags, described on page 24.)*

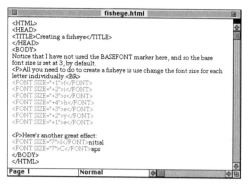

```
                    fisheye.html
<HTML>
<HEAD>
<TITLE>Creating a fisheye</TITLE>
</HEAD>
<BODY>
Notice that I have not used the BASEFONT marker here, and so the base
font size is set at 3, by default.
<P>All you need to do to create a fisheye is use change the font size for each
letter individually.<BR>
<FONT SIZE="+1">f</FONT>
<FONT SIZE="+2">i</FONT>
<FONT SIZE="+3">s</FONT>
<FONT SIZE="+4">h</FONT>
<FONT SIZE="+3">e</FONT>
<FONT SIZE="+2">y</FONT>
<FONT SIZE="+1">e</FONT>

<P>Here's another great effect:
<FONT SIZE="7">I</FONT>nitial
<FONT SIZE="7">C</FONT>aps
</BODY>
</HTML>

Page 1              Normal
```

Figure 2-27. *The big difference between FONT and BASEFONT, as illustrated here, is that FONT can use relative values and depend on the BASEFONT value.*

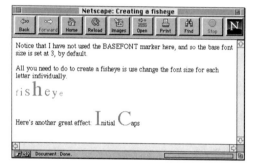

Figure 2-28. *You can create some interesting effects by raising or lowering the font size of individual characters.*

 A good way to make your text stand out is to change the font size of a few characters or a few words.

To change the font size of one or more characters:

1. Type **<FONT**.

2. Type **SIZE="n">** where *n* is a number from 1 to 7. You may also use *+n* and *-n* to denote a value relative to the BASEFONT value. (See preceding page.)

3. Type the text whose font size you wish to change.

4. Type **</FONT>**.

✔ Tips

■ Use the FONT marker to change the font size of just a few characters or a few words. Use BASEFONT to change the font size of the whole document.

■ A value of 3 represents the size that the user has chosen for text in the Preferences dialog box or the default font size used by the browser.

■ You can make fisheye designs by changing the FONT size of each letter in a word in an ascending and then descending pattern.

■ Don't make your body text larger than the headers. This will confuse your users more than help them. It is important to maintain the organizational hierarchy of your page so that the users don't get lost.

Changing the font size

Using BIG and SMALL to change the font size

Standard HTML uses the BIG and SMALL tags to change the relative size of the text. Mosaic recognizes BIG and SMALL but Netscape 1.1 ignores them.

To change font size with BIG and SMALL:

1. Type **<BIG>** or **<SMALL>** before the text that you wish to make bigger or smaller, respectively.

2. Type the text that should be bigger or smaller.

3. Type **</BIG>** or **</SMALL>** according to the tag used in step 1.

✔ Tip

■ You can presently use Netscape *and* standard HTML tags simultaneously so that both browsers recognize the change in font size **(Figures 2-32 and 2-33)**. If and when one of the browsers begins to understand both systems, this method may create undesirable results.

Figure 2-29. *The BIG and SMALL tags are part of the standard version of HTML 3.*

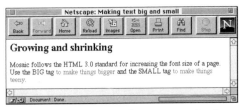

Figure 2-30. *Netscape 1.1 does not recognize the BIG and SMALL tags. However, you may change the font size for pages browsed with Netscape by using BASEFONT and SIZE. (See pages 22-23.)*

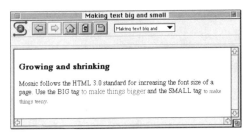

Figure 2-31. *Mosaic correctly interprets the BIG and SMALL tags.*

Figure 2-32. *So that both Netscape and Mosaic users see the font size changes, use both Netscape's BASEFONT and FONT tags as well as Standard HTML's BIG and SMALL tags (understood by Mosaic) in the same HTML document.*

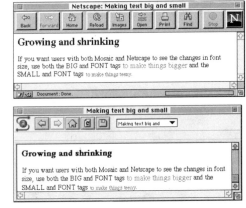

Figure 2-33. *Each browser understands one set of tags and the result is thus the same in both browsers.*

Figure 2-34. *Although you can include an image in your blinking definition, so to speak, only the text will blink.*

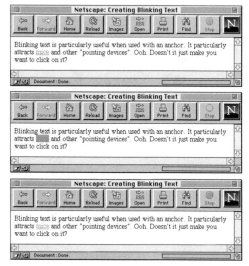

Figure 2-35. *Blinking text appears normal (top), then highlighted in a lighter shade (middle), and then normal again (bottom).*

Making text blink

NETSCAPE ONLY Another way to make text stand out is to make it blink. You can apply the BLINK tag to anchors, links or any important text that you have on the page.

To make text blink:

1. Type **<BLINK>**.

2. Type the text that you want to blink.

3. Type **</BLINK>**.

✔ Tips

■ In this age of graphic interfaces, blinking text virtually cries out to be clicked on. If you use blinking text for anything but a link, you may frustrate or confuse your user.

■ You can include an image in your blinking definition, but it won't blink.

■ Blinking text blinks in a slightly lighter shade of its normal color. A blinking URL that the user has not visited, for example, will blink in shades of blue, while normal text will blink in shades of gray.

■ You may not use blinking text in the TITLE.

Making text blink

Changing the color of body text

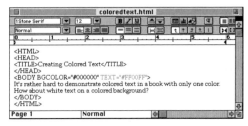

Figure 2-36. *Remember to select a text color that works well with your background color. (If you don't specify the background color, the background will be gray, by default.)*

The TEXT marker gives you, the designer, the power to change the color of the text. Although this is not widely accepted among browsers, and will not be appreciated by users with black and white or grayscale monitors, it can be a powerful design tool.

To change the color of the text:

1. Inside the BODY marker, type **TEXT="#rrggbb"**, where *rr* is replaced by the hexadecimal Red component, *gg* is the hexadecimal Green component and *bb* is the hexadecimal Blue component.

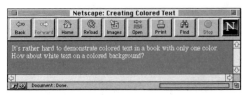

Figure 2-37. *Although this example is pretty basic, you can see that changing the color of your text can give your web pages an immediate impact.*

The TEXT marker must be placed inside the BODY marker. (The full tag may read something like <BODY TEXT="#FFFFFF"> for white text.)

✔ Tips

■ See Appendix B and the inside back cover for a complete listing of hexadecimal values and common color representations.

■ You may only choose one color for the entire body text.

■ Be sure to choose complementary colors for your background and links that work well with your body text color. (See pages 27 and 55.)

■ Check your page on a monochrome monitor before distributing it. What looks good in color may be impossible to read in grays.

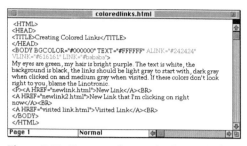

Figure 2-38. *You may select a color for new links, visited links and active links (one that is being clicked).*

Figure 2-39. *It is important to choose colors (or shades of gray, as in this example) that have enough contrast so that you can see all the items on the page, but not so much (especially with colors) as to be garish and distracting.*

Changing the color of links

The LINK markers let you change the color of links or anchors. Since certain standard link colors have already been established—like blue for links that have not yet been visited—you should be careful not to confuse your user with inopportune color choices.

To change the color of your links:

1. Place the cursor inside the BODY marker, after *BODY* but before the >.

2. To change the color of links that have not yet been visited, type **LINK="#rrggbb"**, where *rr* is replaced by the hexadecimal Red component, *gg* is the hexadecimal Green component and *bb* is the hexadecimal Blue component. The default is LINK="#0000FF".

3. To change the color of links that have been already been visited, type **VLINK="#rrggbb"**, where *rr* is replaced by the hexadecimal Red component, *gg* is the hexadecimal Green component and *bb* is the hexadecimal Blue component. The default is VLINK="#FF00FF".

4. To change the color of a link when the user clicks on it, type **ALINK="#rrggbb"**, where *rr* is replaced by the hexadecimal Red component, *gg* is the hexadecimal Green component and *bb* is the hexadecimal Blue component. The default is ALINK="#FF0000".

Changing the color of links

✔ Tips

■ You may only choose one color for each type of link. Make this choice inside the BODY marker.

■ See Appendix B and the inside back cover for a complete listing of hexadecimal values and the equivalents for many common colors.

■ Netscape's Fonts and Colors Preferences dialog box lets the users choose to use the colors you have chosen (Let Document Override) or to always use the color they have chosen (Always Use Mine).

■ Make sure you test the colors of your text, links and background together. Also test your color page on a black and white and a grayscale monitor. Your color choices may not have enough contrast to be distinguishable from each other **(Figure 2-41)**. This could be disastrous if your text or links melt into your background color.

■ Don't use different colors for links from page to page. The users won't know what to click on or which pages they've already visited.

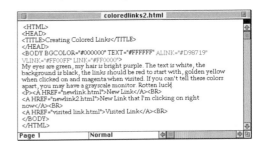

Figure 2-40. *This HTML looks promising enough, and the colors look fine (if a bit discordant) on screen.*

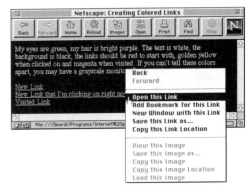

Figure 2-41. *But when shown on a grayscale monitor (or in a grayscale book like this one), the difference between the colors is too slight and will be lost on the user.*

Changing the color of links

IMAGES

Programs used in examples

In this chapter I use Adobe Photoshop to work with images. It is the best all around image editing program and is available for several operating systems, including Macintosh and Windows.

If you don't have Photoshop, I recommend the shareware program Graphic-Converter for Macintosh. For Windows, try LViewPro.

Perhaps the greatest appeal of the World Wide Web and of HTML documents in particular is that they can contain colorful images. You can insert a photo of your cat on your personal home page, or a representation of your company's logo on your business page. You can add images to link definitions, making buttons that take your reader to their next destination. You can use custom icons in lists or use miniature images to point to larger ones. And perhaps most exciting of all, you can create images with more than one hot spot, so that a click in one area brings the user to point A while a click in a different area brings the user to point B.

Image formats

The Web is accessed every day by millions of Macs, Windows-based PCs, Unix machines and other kinds of computers. The graphics you use in your Web page must be in a format that each of these operating systems can recognize. Presently, the two most widely used formats on the Web are GIF and JPEG. Most browsers can view GIF inline images; Netscape 2 can also view JPEG images inline.

GIF Format

GIF, or Graphics Interchange Format, was developed by CompuServe for platform independent images on its online service. Its use of LZW compression reduces the size of images with large blocks of the same color—which are common in computer generated art. In addition, LZW is a lossless compression scheme. You can compress, uncompress and recompress the image again and again without any loss in quality.

JPEG Compression

The JPEG compression scheme is ideal for photographs and other "natural" color images. JPEG compressed images may have millions of colors, and their file size is determined primarily by their image size, not their number of colors.

However, JPEG is "lossy" compression—deciding that the eye cannot distinguish as many colors as are in your original image, it may eliminate them permanently to save space. Uncompressing the image will not restore the lost data. Most programs that let you save images with JPEG compression allow you to control the ratio between data loss and image compression.

Figure 3-1. *Logotypes and other computer generated images, or images with few colors should be saved in GIF format.*

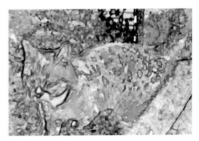

Figure 3-2. *Full-color photographs and other* naturally *created images, or images with more than 256 colors should be saved in JPEG format.*

Image formats

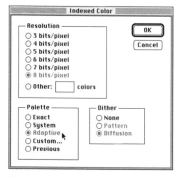

Figure 3-3. *Select Indexed Color from Photoshop's Mode menu before saving in CompuServe GIF format.*

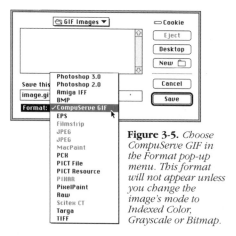

Figure 3-4. *Choose 8 bits/pixel (or less) and an Adaptive palette.*

Figure 3-5. *Choose CompuServe GIF in the Format pop-up menu. This format will not appear unless you change the image's mode to Indexed Color, Grayscale or Bitmap.*

GIF format

Use the GIF format for logos, banners and other computer generated images. GIF images are limited to 256 colors or less.

To save an image in GIF format:

1. Open the image with Photoshop, or the desired image editing program.

2. Select Indexed Color (for color images) in the Mode menu **(Figure 3-3)**. (You can also save GIF images in Grayscale and Bitmap modes.)

3. In the Indexed Color dialog box that appears, choose 8 bits/pixel (or fewer) under Resolution, Adaptive for Palette, and Diffusion for Dither **(Figure 3-4)**.

4. Select Save as in the File menu.

5. Choose CompuServe GIF in the Format menu **(Figure 3-5)**.

6. Click OK.

✔ Tips

■ Photoshop's Adaptive palette collects colors from the more commonly used areas of the color spectrum that appear in the image. That is, if your image is mostly red and orange, most of the colors in an Adaptive palette will be red and orange.

■ You can also use the GIF89a Export plug-in for Photoshop to create GIF images. You can find the plug-in at *http://www.adobe.com/*

GIF format

JPEG compression

Use JPEG for photographs and for images with more than 256 colors.

To save an image with JPEG compression:

1. Open the image with Photoshop, or the desired image editing program.

2. Choose RGB Color or CMYK Color in the Mode menu **(Figure 3-6)**.

Figure 3-6. *A JPEG image may be in either RGB Color or CMYK Color.*

3. Select Save as in the File menu.

4. Choose JPEG in the Format pop-up menu **(Figure 3-7)**.

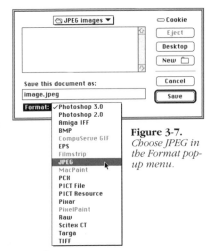

5. Choose the desired quality in the JPEG Options dialog box. You may want to experiment with different values until you get an image with sufficient quality at a file size you (and your users) can live with **(Figure 3-8)**.

Figure 3-7. *Choose JPEG in the Format pop-up menu.*

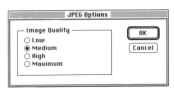

Figure 3-8. *The higher the image quality you choose in the JPEG Options dialog box, the less compression you will achieve.*

JPEG compression

```
        inlineimage.html
<HTML>
<HEAD><TITLE>Inserting an Inline Image</TITLE>
</HEAD>
<H1>Cookie and Woody</H1>
<P>Generally considered the sweetest and yet most independent cats in
the <A HREF=pioneerval.html>Pioneer Valley,</A> Cookie and Woody are
consistently underestimated by their humble humans.
Here's Cookie and Woody, exhausted after helping us pack the last time we
moved:
<P><IMG SRC="catsonbox.gif">
</BODY>
</HTML>
Page 1               Normal
```

Figure 3-9. *Use a <P> before your image definition to start it on its own line.*

Figure 3-10. *Images are aligned to the left side of the page, by default. Unless you use the align attributes (pages 49–50), you can't wrap the text around the image.*

Inline images

Inline images are those that appear automatically with the surrounding text when the user jumps to your Web page.

To place an inline image on your page:

1. Place the cursor where you want the image to appear.

2. Type **<IMG SRC="image.location"** where *image.location* shows the location of the image file on the server.

3. If desired, type **ALT="substitute text"** where *substitute text* is what the user will see if they can't view images with their browser or if they have temporarily turned off image viewing to speed up processing.

4. Type the final **>**.

✔ Tips

- Use small images to keep the page's loading time to a minimum. Don't expect your users to wait more than 30 seconds to load and view your page (about 30K total between text and images with a 14.4 Kbps modem connection).

- Use icons to point to images too large for your page. (See page 36.)

- Use alternative text for browsers, like Lynx, that don't support images. (See page 34.)

Alternative text

Some browsers do not support images at all. Other browsers support them but the user may have such a slow connection that they choose not to view the images, or to load them in manually. You can create text that will appear if the image, for whatever reason, does not.

Some browsers, like Lynx, that do not support images, are used by the blind because they can speak the contents to the user. This is just one more reason to add alternative text to your images.

To provide alternative text when images don't appear:

1. Place the cursor where you want the image (or alternative text) to appear.

2. Type **<IMG SRC="image.gif"** where *image.gif* is the location of the image on the server.

3. Type **ALT="**.

4. Type the text that should appear if, for some reason, the image itself does not.

5. Type **">**.

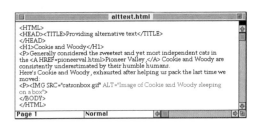

Figure 3-11. *If your alternative text contains one or more spaces, you must enclose it in quotation marks.*

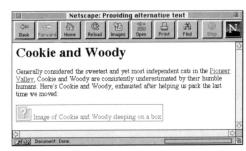

Figure 3-12. *The alternative text will appear if the image cannot be found, if the user has deselected Autoload images, or if the browser does not support images.*

Alternative text

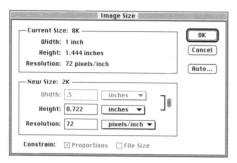

Figure 3-13. *Check the Proportions and uncheck the File Size options in the Image Size dialog box. Then, with* inches *selected, type the new width in the Width box.*

Figure 3-14. *The original image (shown above at 91% of its normal size so I could fit it on the page) and the corresponding icon (at left at full size).*

External images

If you want to give your users access to a large image without compelling them to wait for it to load every time they read your Web page, you can create a small icon with a link to the larger image. This way, the user can choose to see the larger image or just continue with your Web page.

To create a small icon of your image:

1. Open your large image in Photoshop, or other image editing program.

2. Select Image Size in the Image menu.

3. Check the Proportions option and make sure the File Size option is unchecked **(Figure 3-13)**.

4. Select inches in the pop-up menu to the right of Width **(Figure 3-13)**.

5. Type **.5** in the Width box (or what-ever smaller size you wish). The Height will be adjusted automatically **(Figure 3-13)**.

6. Select Save as in the File menu.

7. Type a new name for the icon, so you don't replace the full size image.

External images

Linking icons to external images

Once you have created the icon of your large image and given it a separate name, you can add the information to your HTML page so the user can first view the small image and then access the larger image if they wish.

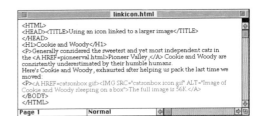

Figure 3-15. *Remember to use the full size image in the link and the icon in the image definition.*

To link the small icon to your larger image:

1. Place the cursor in your HTML page where you wish the icon to be placed.

2. Type **<A HREF="image.location">**, where *image.location* is the location of the full sized image on your server.

3. Type **<IMG SRC="icon.location"**, where *icon.location* is the location of your icon on the server.

4. If desired, type **ALT="alternative text"**, where *alternative text* is the text that should appear if, for some reason, the icon does not.

5. Type the final **>** of the icon definition.

6. Type the clickable text that you wish to accompany the icon. It's a good idea to include the actual size in K of the full sized image so the user knows what they're getting into by clicking it.

7. Type **</A>** to complete the link to the full sized image.

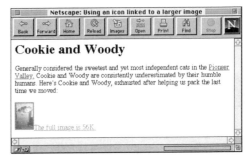

Figure 3-16. *In this example, the icon is 2K and takes 2 seconds to load. The user can choose to view the larger image or to continue reading the page.*

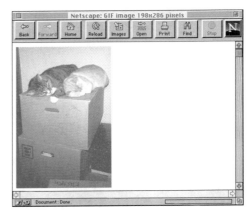

Figure 3-17. *When the user clicks on the icon, Netscape opens a new window with the full size image.*

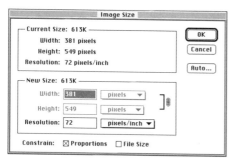

Figure 3-18. *Select pixels in the Width and Height pop-up menus and write down the values shown (in this example, 381 and 549).*

```
                    size.html
<HTML>
<HEAD><TITLE>Using a low resolution image to speed up
viewing</TITLE>
</HEAD>
<H1>The Four Sisters</H1>
<P>The Four Sisters Corporaton was begun by the previously unknown
four sisters. Here's a rare photo:
<P><IMG WIDTH=381 HEIGHT=549 SRC="038@72.jpeg" ALT="The Four
Sisters">
</BODY>
</HTML>
Page 1            Normal
```

Figure 3-19. *If you specify the exact height and width values in pixels, Netscape won't have to spend time doing it and will display the image more quickly.*

Figure 3-20. *The image at its original size.*

Optimizing images for speedier viewing

NETSCAPE ONLY Netscape has several extensions that help your images load more quickly. Specifying the image's dimensions lets Netscape fill in the text around the image before loading the entire image (and verifying its file size). If you create a low resolution image, Netscape can load it first, and let your users browse as it loads the higher resolution image. Finally, if you interlace your images, Netscape can load them gradually—allowing the user to see the image as it appears, and interact with the image immediately.

To specify the size of your image:

1. Open the image in Photoshop, or other image editing program.

2. Select Image Size in the Image menu.

3. Choose pixels for the Unit of measure in both the Width and Height text boxes **(Figure 3-18)**.

4. Write down the values shown in the Width and Height text boxes.

5. In your HTML document where you wish the image to appear, type **<IMG SRC="image.location"**, where *image.location* is the location of the image on the server.

6. Type **WIDTH=x HEIGHT=y>**, using the values you jotted down in step 4 to specify the values for *x* and *y* (the width and height of your image) in pixels. See page 53 for more information on using WIDTH and HEIGHT to scale images.

7. Add other image attributes as desired and then type the final **>**.

Optimizing images

Creating low resolution images

 You can make life more pleasant for your user by creating a low resolution image that Netscape can show immediately while it takes its time loading the higher resolution image.

To create a low resolution version of your image:

1. Open your image in Photoshop, or other image editing program.

2. Select Image Size in the Image menu **(Figure 3-21)**.

3. Check File Size and Proportions in the Image Size dialog box. **(Figure 3-22)**.

4. Change the value of Resolution to 72 dpi or lower and click OK **(Figure 3-22)**.

5. Choose Save as in the File menu and save the low resolution image with a new name.

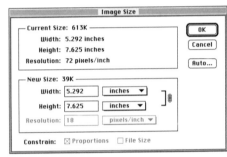

Figure 3-21. *Choose Image Size in the Image menu.*

Figure 3-22. *With Proportions checked and File Size unchecked, change the value in the Resolution box, preferably to a number that divides evenly into 72 (like 36, 18 or even 9).*

Creating low resolution images

Figure 3-23. *The HEIGHT and WIDTH attributes are discussed on page 53. They are necessary here to show both images at the proper size.*

Figure 3-24. *The low resolution image is replaced gradually by the higher resolution image. The call out line marks the division between the two. The status information in the lower left corner shows how much more time it will take to finish loading the high resolution image. Without the lower resolution image, the user would have to wait all that time before seeing* anything.

Using low resolution images

Once you have created a low resolution version of your image, all you need to do is reference it in your HTML document.

To use a low resolution version of an image:

1. Create a low resolution version of your image. (See preceding page.)

2. Place the cursor where you want the full resolution image to appear.

3. Type **<IMG SRC="image.gif"** where *image.gif* is the location on the server of the high resolution image.

4. Type **LOWSRC="imagelow.gif"** where *imagelow.gif* is the location on the server of the low resolution image.

5. Type **HEIGHT=x WIDTH=y**, where *x* and *y* are the height and width in pixels, respectively. If you do not specify these values, Netscape uses the size of the smaller (low resolution) image for both images.

6. If desired, type **ALT="substitute text"** where *substitute text* is the text that will appear if the user can't view images with their browser or if they have temporarily turned off image viewing to speed up processing.

7. Type the final **>**.

Using low resolution images

Interlacing GIF images

Interlacing an image prepares it so that a browser (presently, only Netscape) can show it at gradually increasing resolutions. Although the initial image is blurry, the user does not have to wait for the finished image to appear. Instead, the user can scroll around the page and then return when the image is complete.

The shareware GraphicConverter, written by Thorsten Lemke is ideal for converting graphics file formats but also has a good interlacing feature. (You can also use Photoshop's new GIF89a Export plug-in.)

To interlace an image:

1. Open the image with GraphicConverter.

2. Select Save as in the File menu. The Save as dialog box appears.

3. Choose GIF in the Format submenu in the upper right area of the dialog box **(Figure 3-25)**.

4. Click the Options button.

5. Choose 89a in the Version section and Interlaced in the Row Order section of the GIF Options dialog box that appears **(Figure 3-26)**.

6. Click OK and then Save.

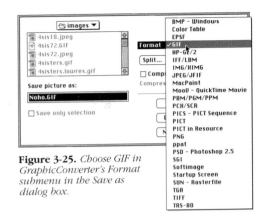

Figure 3-25. *Choose GIF in GraphicConverter's Format submenu in the Save as dialog box.*

Figure 3-26. *Check 89a under Version, Interlaced under Row Order and Optimize under Depth (this last is a free bonus option that automatically chooses the minimum bit depth—and thus file size—according to the image's current number of colors).*

Figure 3-27. *Netscape shows the interlaced image gradually, allowing the user to browse around the page and read the text while the image comes into full view.*

Image Size

If you've wandered a bit around the Internet, you are sure to have experienced The Page From Hell. The designer was so anxious to show you every image he's ever created, that he placed them all on the same page. And no small images either—these are 24 bit color images. You're still on a 14.4 modem, but that's no excuse to make you wait this long to see the page. After a minute or two staring at the progress indicator at the bottom of your browser, you bag, and surf to a more friendlier page.

When you construct *your* page, make sure you keep the entire page to under 30K—including images. It will take your users with 14.4 modems, not to mention those who are still on 9600s, about a second to load each K of data, for a total of 30 seconds. That's about how long you can expect anyone to wait.

If you want to include larger images, you have several options. First , you can use a miniature version, or icon, of the image on your page that links the user—if they so choose—to the full image (page 36). Next, you can create a low resolution version of the image that loads almost immediately and allows the user to browse while the high resolution image is loading (pages 38–39). Finally, you can interlace the image which also lets the user browse almost immediately as the image gradually comes into focus (page 40). If your pages are still interminably slow, try dividing your images among several pages.

Why the resolution is not important

Since most monitors display everything at 72 dpi, there is no reason to save your images with a higher resolution, unless you want your users to be able to download and print your images at the other end. Generally, that's not necessary, and the higher resolution only guarantees longer download times.

Why the number of colors *is* important

Although many Macintoshes and some higher-end monitors for PCs can show thousands or even millions of colors on the screen at once, the vast majority of users are limited to 256 colors. This means that if you create several images and each uses its own set of 256 colors, the images will not appear correctly. Therefore, if you plan to include several images on a single page, you need to be careful to either limit each image to 50 or so colors, or to use the same set of colors for every image.

In addition, the fewer the colors in your image, the smaller the file size, and thus the faster the download time. To create a fast, friendly Web page, keep your color count to a minimum.

Size, resolution and colors

Reducing the colors

A GIF image's size is directly related to the number of colors it has. It can have at most 256 colors, and if you can reduce the number even further, you can save considerably on load time and user patience.

To reduce the number of colors with Photoshop:

1. Open the image with Adobe Photoshop.

2. Select Indexed Color in the Mode menu **(Figure 3-28)**.

3. In the Indexed Color dialog box, select the 8 bits/pixel option in the Resolution section and Adaptive in the Palette section **(Figure 3-29)**.

4. Click OK and save the document.

✔ Tip

■ If there is a number in the Other box under Resolution when you open the dialog box, you should use the Exact palette.

To reduce the number of colors with GraphicConverter:

1. Open the image with GraphicConverter.

2. Select Minimize Color Table in the Colors submenu of the Picture menu. GraphicConverter uses the smallest possible color depth to accommodate the number of colors used, which can result in a sizable savings **(Figure 3-30)**.

3. Save the document.

Figure 3-28. *Choose Indexed color in the Mode menu.*

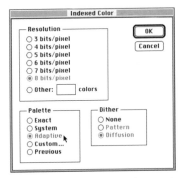

Figure 3-29. *Choose a Resolution of 8 bits/pixel or less.*

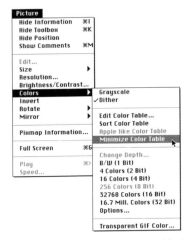

Figure 3-30. *GraphicConverter's Minimize Color Table option in the Colors submenu in the Picture menu automatically reduces the color depth of the image, thereby reducing its file size.*

Reducing the colors

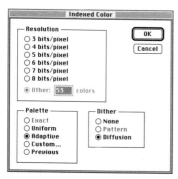

Figure 3-31. *If there is no number in the Other box, the image has at least 256 colors and perhaps more.*

Counting colors

Once you have reduced the colors in your image with the Indexed Colors option, you can count the colors in your image.

To count the colors in an image with Photoshop:

1. Open the image in Photoshop or other image editing program.

2. Select RGB in the Mode menu.

3. Select Indexed Color in the Mode menu.

4. The Other: box shows exactly how many colors there are in the image **(Figure 3-31)**. You may change the number if you wish.

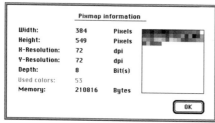

Figure 3-32. *You can only view the information in GraphicConverter's Pixmap information dialog box. To change the number of colors, see the preceding page.*

To count colors with GraphicConverter:

1. Open the image with GraphicConverter.

2. Select Pixmap information in the Picture menu. The second to last item in the Pixmap information dialog box shows exactly how many colors you have used in the document while the color table on the right side of the dialog box shows the individual colors themselves **(Figure 3-32)**.

3. Click OK.

Counting colors

Viewing and editing the color table

If you want to see which colors are being used in your image, you can look at the image's color table.

To look at and edit the colors in an image with Photoshop:

1. Open the image in Photoshop, or other image editing program.

2. Select Indexed Color in the Mode menu if you haven't already done so.

3. Select 8 bits/pixel in the Resolution section and Adaptive in the Palette section.

4. Select Color Table in the Mode menu. The Color Table dialog box appears showing you each color that is used in the image **(Figure 3-33)**.

5. Click a color to see its RGB, HSL, Lab or CYMK values. You can change the color by entering different values in the various text boxes **(Figure 3-34)**.

6. Click OK. If you've modified the color, the corresponding areas in the image with that color will automatically change to the new color.

✔ Tips

■ Grayscale images do not have a color table. If you have a grayscale image and you want to count the number of grays used, convert the image to Indexed Color.

■ GraphicConverter works essentially the same as Photoshop for editing color tables.

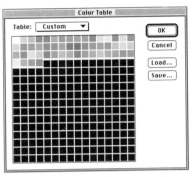

Figure 3-33. *The black squares indicate unused colors. In this example, the image contains only 53 colors.*

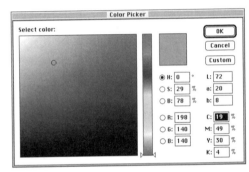

Figure 3-34. *Changing a color in the color table with the Color picker changes each area in the image that had the original color.*

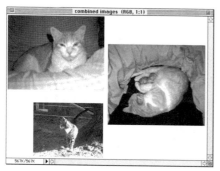

Figure 3-35. *The only way to ensure that each image shares the same color table is to combine them in one document and then apply the Indexed Color command.*

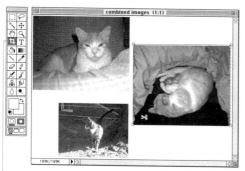

Figure 3-36. *The crop tool (left) can cut out part of an image while retaining all of the original image's properties, including color mode and color table.*

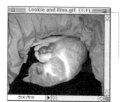

Figure 3-37. *Be sure and save the new file with a new name so that you don't replace the* combined images *file.*

Common color tables

In order to use the maximum number of colors without fear of running over the limit of 256 (see page 41), use the same color table for each image.

Using the same color table in several images:

1. In Photoshop, or some other image editing program, create one large image that is large enough to hold each of your individual images.

2. Either create or copy the individual images into the larger one **(Figure 3-35)**.

3. Select Indexed Color in the Mode menu, and 8 bits/pixel under Resolution (or less) and Adaptive under Palette in the dialog box that appears. This is the only way to ensure that you are limiting the collection of images to a maximum of 256 colors.

4. Save the document with a name like "combined images".

5. With the cropping tool, cut out one of the individual images (**Fig. 3-36**).

6. Save the new reduced image with a new name (**Figure 3-37**).

7. Open the *combined images* file and repeat steps 5 and 6 for each individual image.

Common color tables

✔ Tips

■ Although it seems like you should be able to save the Color Table (using the Save button in the Color Table dialog box) and then load it into each smaller image, the result is not quite what you'd expect. In fact, since there is no way to map which colors go to which parts of the image, the result is quite ugly. Try it.

■ If you are drawing new images from scratch, there is another way to make sure that each image shares a common color table. After creating the first image, save its color table by clicking the Save button in the Color Table dialog box and giving the table file a name. Then, create a new empty file and, before actually drawing the image, load in the color table from the first image. Repeat the process for each new image.

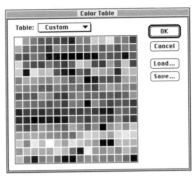

Figure 3-38. *Once you have created the individual images, each image will share the same color table, and thus will be sure to display correctly on screen.*

Figure 3-39. *Select the image itself, using the lasso or other selection tools.*

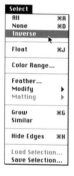

Figure 3-40. *Use the Inverse command in the Select menu to select everything but the image, that is, the background.*

— *Default Colors control*

Figure 3-41. *Once you've inverted the selection, click the Default Colors control and then the Delete key to change the background to one solid color, in this case, white.*

Using transparency

You can make the background of your images transparent so that they float seamlessly above the page. You can also convert one of the colors in your images into transparency to create special effects.

Before you make the background transparent, make sure that it's all the same color. Otherwise, only parts of the background will be affected when you make it transparent.

To make the background a solid color:

1. Open the image in Photoshop, or another image editing program.

2. Use the Lasso and other selection tools to select everything except the background **(Figure 3-39)**.

3. Select Inverse in the Selection menu to select only the background **(Figure 3-40)**.

4. Click the Default Colors control in the tool box to reset the foreground color to black and the background color to white **(Figure 3-41)**, or click the background color to set it to the color of your choice.

5. Press Delete to change the color of the selected area (the background) to the current background color **(Figure 3-41)**.

6. Save the image.

To make the image's background transparent:

Photoshop's long awaited GIF89a Export plugin is great for creating transparency. You can also use GraphicConverter (for Mac), LView Pro (for Windows), or some other utility.

1. Create or open an image in Photoshop. Make sure the background is all the same color and that the image is in Indexed color mode.

2. Choose GIF89a Export in the Export submenu in the File menu **(Figure 3-42)**. If this option does not appear in your menu, you either don't have the GIF plug-in or you don't have it installed correctly.

3. In the GIF 89a Export dialog box that appears, click the color(s) in the image that you want to make transparent **(Figure 3-43)**.

4. Click OK and give the file a name.

✔ Tips

■ You can find the GIF 89a Export plug-in at Adobe's home page (*http://www.adobe.com/*) or in their forum on CompuServe (*Go Adobeapps*).

■ Hold down the Command (or Alt) key and click to restore colors to their original state.

■ You can export GIF images directly from an RGB image. In this case, the transparency is created from a mask.

■ You may create a selection before selecting the GIF 89a Export plugin and then use that selection to create transparency by choosing it in the Transparency From pop-up menu in the GIF 89a Export dialog box.

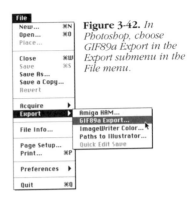

Figure 3-42. *In Photoshop, choose GIF89a Export in the Export submenu in the File menu.*

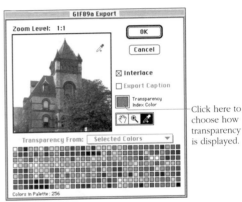

Click here to choose how transparency is displayed.

Figure 3-43. *Click on colors with the eyedropper until the desired area is transparent. To restore colors hold down the Command/Alt key and click.*

Figure 3-44. *Include the image in your HTML code in the normal way and what used to be white is now completely invisible against the gray background.*

Figure 3-45. When you align an image to the right, you are actually wrapping text to the left (and vice versa).

Figure 3-46. Both Netscape (middle screen) and Mosaic (bottom) can wrap text around images.

Wrapping text around images

You can use the ALIGN attribute (with the *left* and *right* variables only) to wrap text around an image. (Yes, these really should have their own attribute, like WRAP, instead of ALIGN which seems like it should do something rather different—which it does on page 54.)

To wrap text around one side of an image:

1. Type **<IMG SRC="image.location"** where *image.location* indicates the location of the image on the server.

2. *Either* type **ALIGN=left** to align the image to the left of the screen while the text flows to the right *or* type **ALIGN=right** to align the image to the right edge of the screen while the text flows on the left side of the image.

3. Add other image attributes, as described in other parts of this chapter, if desired.

4. Type the final **>**.

5. Type the text that should flow next to the image.

To wrap text between two images:

1. Type **<IMG SRC="right.image" ALIGN=right>** where *right.image* indicates the location on the server of the image that should appear on the right side of the screen.

2. Type **<IMG SRC="left.image" ALIGN=left>** where *left.image* indicates the location on the server of the image that should appear on the left side of the screen.

3. Type the text that should flow between the two images.

✔ Tips

■ Each image will continue to push the text to one side until it either encounters a break (see page 51) or until there is no more text **(Figure 3-48)**.

■ The images don't necessarily have to come one after another. The key is to place each image *directly before* the text it should "disrupt" **(Figures 3-49 and 3-50)**.

Figure 3-47. *To flow text between two images, first define the images one after another, then add the text.*

Figure 3-48. *In Netscape, as soon as the text passes the image boundaries (where the word* Northampton *begins), the remaining text reverts to its original alignment. In Mosaic, the word* Northampton *would appear aligned under the* V *in* Valley.

Figure 3-49. *By changing the position of the left image's HTML code, you can choose where it begins on the page.*

Figure 3-50. *The left image displaces the first text it encounters, which in this case is "This triplex...".*

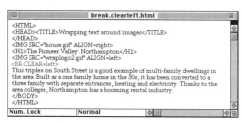

```
break.clearleft.html
<HTML>
<HEAD><TITLE>Wrapping text around images</TITLE>
</HEAD>
<IMG SRC="house.gif" ALIGN=right>
<H1>The Pioneer Valley: Northampton</H1>
<IMG SRC="wraplogo2.gif" ALIGN=left>
<BR CLEAR=left>
This triplex on South Street is a good example of multi-family dwellings in
the area. Built as a one family home in the 30s, it has been converted to a
three family with separate entrances, heating and electricity. Thanks to the
area colleges, Northampton has a booming rental industry.
</BODY>
</HTML>
Num. Lock          Normal
```

Figure 3-51. *Notice the order: first comes the image of the house, then the header, then the logo, then the paragraph.*

Figure 3-52. *The Clear=left attribute makes the text stop flowing until it reaches an empty left margin (that is, below the bottom of the left-aligned image).*

Stopping text wrap

A wrapped image affects all the text that follows it, unless you insert a special line break. The CLEAR attribute added to the regular BR tag indicates that the text should not begin until the specified margin is clear (that is, at the end of the image or images).

To stop the text from wrapping:

1. Create your image and the text as described on page 31.

2. Place the cursor where you want to stop wrapping text to the side of the image.

3. *Either* type **<BR CLEAR=left>** to stop flowing text until there are no more images aligned to the left margin, *or* type **<BR CLEAR=right>** to stop flowing text until there are no more images aligned to the right margin, *or* type **<BR CLEAR=all>** to stop flowing text until there are no more images on either margin.

```
break.clearall.html
<HTML>
<HEAD><TITLE>Wrapping text around images</TITLE>
</HEAD>
<IMG SRC="house.gif" ALIGN=right>
<H1>The Pioneer Valley: Northampton</H1>
<IMG SRC="wraplogo2.gif" ALIGN=left>
<BR CLEAR=all>
This triplex on South Street is a good example of multi-family dwellings in
the area. Built as a one family home in the 30s, it has been converted to a
three family with separate entrances, heating and electricity. Thanks to the
area colleges, Northampton has a booming rental industry.
</BODY>
</HTML>
494 Chars          Normal
```

Figure 3-53. *The order is the same as in the last example; only the CLEAR attribute has changed.*

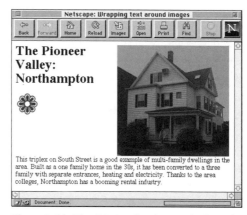

Figure 3-54. *The CLEAR=all code stops the flow of text until all images have been passed.*

Adding space around an image

NETSCAPE ONLY Look carefully at the image in Figure 3-55. If you don't want your text butting right up to the image, you can use the Netscape extensions VSPACE and HSPACE to add a buffer around your image.

To add space around an image:

1. Type **<IMG SRC="image.location"** where *image.location* indicates the location on the server of your image.

2. Type **HSPACE=x** where *x* is the number of pixels of space to add on *both* the right and left sides of the image.

3. Type **VSPACE=x** where *x* is the number of pixels of space to add on *both* the top and bottom of the image.

4. Add other image attributes as desired and type the final **>**.

✔ Tips

■ You don't have to add both HSPACE and VSPACE at the same time.

■ If you just want to add space to one side of the image, use Photoshop to add blank space to that side, and skip HSPACE and VSPACE altogether. Then, make the blank space transparent. (See pages 47–48.)

Figure 3-55. *Netscape has a bad habit of cramming text right up next to images.*

Figure 3-56. *You can add either HSPACE or VSPACE, or both, to your images.*

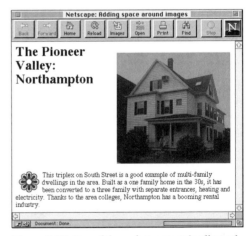

Figure 3-57. *One of the unfortunate side effects of VSPACE is that it adds space both to the top and to the bottom of an image. Although the lower paragraph is no longer jammed against the house, the words* The Pioneer *are no longer aligned with the top of the image.*

Figure 3-58. *The image's original size is revealed in Photoshop by holding down the Option key and clicking in the lower left corner of the window.*

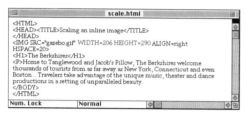

Figure 3-59. *Use dimensions that are multiples of the original size to keep the image in proportion.*

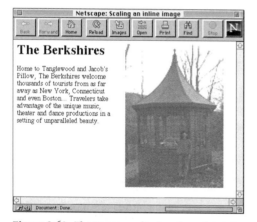

Figure 3-60. *The image quality is not great, but it loads twice as fast as a regular sized image.*

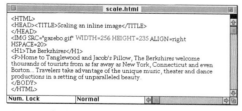

Figure 3-61 (above and right). *You can distort an image to fit nicely with the text as I've done here, but beware: other browsers with other settings may quickly undo your adjustments.*

Scaling an image

NETSCAPE ONLY Netscape lets you change the size of an image just by specifying a new height and width in pixels. This is a great way to have large images on your page without long loading times. Beware, though, if you enlarge your pictures too much, they'll be grainy and ugly.

To scale an image:

1. Type **<IMG SRC="image.location"**, where *image.location* is the location on the server of the image.

2. Type **WIDTH=x HEIGHT=y** where *x* and *y* are the desired width and height, respectively, in pixels, of your image.

3. Add any other image attributes as desired and then type the final **>**.

✔ Tips

■ Don't use the WIDTH and HEIGHT extensions to *reduce* the image size. Instead, create a smaller image. It will load faster and look better.

■ The WIDTH and HEIGHT values don't have to be proportional—you can stretch or elongate an image for a "special" effect **(Figure 3-61)**.

Scaling an image

Aligning images

Perhaps, the more expected use of Netscape's ALIGN extension is for aligning images with text. You can align an image in various ways to a single line in a paragraph. However, be careful with multiple images on the same line—different ALIGN options may have different effects depending on which image is taller and which appears first.

To align an image with text:

1. Type **<IMG SRC="image.location"** where *image.location* indicates the location on the server of the image.

2. Type **ALIGN=direction** where *direction* is one of the attributes described in Figure 3-63: *texttop, top, middle, absmiddle, bottom, baseline* or *absbottom.*

3. Add other attributes as desired and then type the final **>**.

4. Type the text with which you wish to align the image. (This text may also precede the image.)

✔ Tips

■ You may not align an image and wrap text around it at the same time.

■ Mosaic only recognizes the top, middle and bottom values for ALIGN.

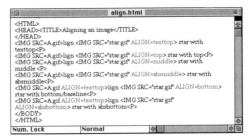

Figure 3-62. *It's important to note that the letter A is an image, not an actual letter. It is aligned with the bottom of the text in the top four examples, and with the top of the text in the last two examples.*

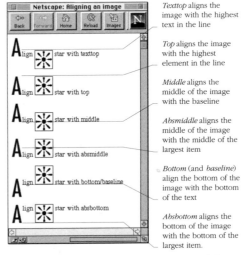

Texttop aligns the image with the highest text in the line

Top aligns the image with the highest element in the line

Middle aligns the middle of the image with the baseline

Absmiddle aligns the middle of the image with the middle of the largest item

Bottom (and *baseline*) align the bottom of the image with the bottom of the text

Absbottom aligns the bottom of the image with the bottom of the largest item.

Figure 3-63. *There are four elements on each line: an image of the letter A, some text, a star, and some more text. The six possible alignment positions are illustrated with the star.*

```
coloredback.html
<HTML>
<HEAD>
<TITLE>Creating a colored background</TITLE>
</HEAD>
<BODY BGCOLOR="#FF00FF">
You can change the color of the background of your page--but make sure
your users can still read the text on top of it. That is the point, right?
</BODY>
</HTML>
Num. Lock          Normal
```

Figure 3-64. *Use the BACKGROUND tag to set the background color. Check the inside back cover and Appendix B for a listing of the most common colors and their hexadecimal equivalents.*

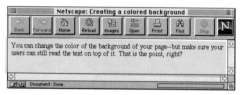

Figure 3-65. *Take my word for it, this page is bright pink!*

Using background color

Tired of basic gray? Netscape's BGCOLOR extension lets you set the color of each Web page you create.

To set the background color:

1. In the BODY tag, after the word BODY but before the final >, type **BGCOLOR="#rrggbb"**, where *rr* is the hexadecimal equivalent of the Red component, *gg* is the hexadecimal equivalent of the Green component and *bb* is the hexadecimal equivalent of the Blue component.

See the inside back cover and Appendix B for a list of colors and their hexadecimal equivalents.

2. Add other attributes to the Body (like link and text colors, see pages 26–27) as desired.

✔ Tip

■ Test your page on a grayscale monitor to make sure there is enough contrast between the color you have chosen for the background and the other elements on the page.

Using background images

You can use one image as the backdrop for your entire page. *Backdrop* is the operative word here. A background image should not detract from the readability of your page, but instead make it more attractive.

Figure 3-66. *You can't add extra image attributes (like LOWSRC) to the BODY tag.*

To use a background image:

1. In the BODY tag at the beginning of your HTML document, after the word BODY but before the final >, type **BACKGROUND=**.

2. Type **"bgimage.gif"**, where *bgimage.gif* is the location on the server of the image you want to use for the background of your page.

3. Add other body attributes (like link and text color, see pages 26–27) as desired.

✔ Tips

■ It is especially important to keep your background image files as small as you can. Use as few colors and as low a resolution as possible.

■ With an image editing program, try increasing the brightness and lowering the contrast simultaneously to soften the background image so it doesn't distract from your foreground text and images.

■ Save your user loading time by using the exact same background image on a series of pages. After the image has been loaded for the first page, each subsequent page uses a cached version to load the image much more quickly.

■ Use tiled images. (See next page.)

Figure 3-67. *You probably shouldn't put text on a background image. It's apt to be covered by your page text.*

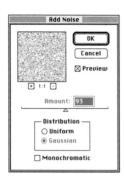

Figure 3-68. *Use the Add noise filter in Photoshop to give your tile an easily combinable background.*

Fig. 3-69. *Create the pattern in your tile.*

Fig. 3-70. *Use the Offset filter to convert the tile into a repeatable pattern.*

```
backtile.html
<HTML><HEAD>
<TITLE>Using an image as a background</TITLE></HEAD>
<BODY BACKGROUND="tile.gif">
You can also use an image for the background. Make sure the images are as
small as possible. Your users won't wait forever. <P>
<FONT SIZE=+3>
<UL><STRONG>Starsearch Enterprises Web page</STRONG><P>
<LI>New products<P>
<LI>Press Releases<P>
<LI>PSO Scheduled<P>
<LI>Job Opportunities at SE<P>
</UL>
</FONT>
</BODY>
</HTML>
Num. Lock          Normal
```

Figure 3-71. *There is no difference in the HTML code between using one image for the background and tiling an image several times for the background. Netscape decides how to treat an image based on its size.*

Figure 3-72. *Netscape tiles your image as many times as necessary to fill the background.*

Using tiled images

If the image you select for your background is smaller than the user's window, it will be tiled to fill the background. You can tweak the image so that it tiles seamlessly.

To create a tiled background:

1. Create a new image of about 100 x 100 pixels in Photoshop.

2. Choose the Add Noise filter in the Noise submenu in the Filters menu to create a textured background **(Figure 3-68)**.

3. Create the desired pattern **(Figure 3-69)**.

4. Select the Offset filter in the Others submenu in the Filters menu **(Figure 3-70)** to create a repeatable pattern.

5. In the Offset filter dialog box, type 10 in the Horizontal and Vertical fields and click Wrap Around.

6. Click OK.

7. Adjust the interior of the image to make the seams disappear. Do not change the borders once you have used the Offset filter.

8. Use the Hue/Saturation and Brightness/Contrast options to reduce the Contrast and make the image lighter. Make it twice as light as you can stand. It is background, after all.

9. Save the image and define it as a background image as described on the preceding page.

Using tiled images

Creating a banner

Having a newspaper-like banner at the top of every Web page is a good way to link your pages together visually.

To place a banner at the top of each page:

1. Create an image that measures 450 x 100 pixels. You can make it narrower and shorter, but you shouldn't make it much wider. Otherwise it won't fit easily on most screens **(Fig. 3-73)**.

2. After converting it to Indexed color, using the smallest bits/pixel ratio you can stand, save it as a GIF image.

3. Use this exact same image at the top of each of your Web pages, by typing **<IMG SRC="image.name">** where *image.name* is the location on the server of the banner.

By using the same image on each Web page, you create the illusion of a static banner. At the same time, since the image is saved in the cache after it is loaded the first time, it will load almost immediately onto each new page your user jumps to.

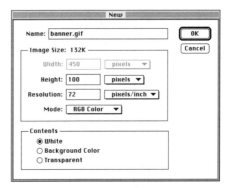

Figure 3-73. When you create your image (here in Photoshop) make sure it is 450 pixels wide, or less.

Figure 3-74. *The only thing special about a banner is that it is the first element in the BODY section.*

Figure 3-75. *Banners appear similarly in Netscape (above) and Mosaic.*

```
                     rule.html
<HTML><HEAD>
<TITLE>Using horizontal rules</TITLE></HEAD>
<BODY>
<IMG SRC="banner.gif" ALT="SE banner">
<H1>New products</H1>
<UL>
<LI>AstroFinder 3
<LI>Pleiades Expander
<LI>Southern Cross
</UL>
<HR SIZE=10 WIDTH=80% ALIGN=center NOSHADE>
</BODY>
</HTML>
Num. Lock          Normal
```

Figure 3-76. *The HR tag includes an automatic line break both before and after the rule.*

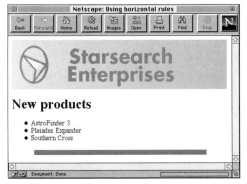

Figure 3-77. *Netscape understands all the HR attributes, which are actually Netscape extensions.*

Figure 3-78. *Mosaic, like most other browsers, understands only the HR tag. It ignores all the attributes.*

Adding horizontal rules

The only graphic element included in HTML version 2 and completely supported by the majority of the browsers is the horizontal rule. Of course, Netscape has added a few attributes, but you should be getting used to that by now.

To insert a horizontal rule:

1. Type **<HR** where you want the rule to appear. The text that follows will appear in a new paragraph below the new rule.

2. NETSCAPE ONLY If desired, type **SIZE=n**, where *n* is the rule's height in pixels.

3. NETSCAPE ONLY If desired, type **WIDTH=w**, where *w* is the width of the rule in pixels, or is a percentage of the width of the document.

4. NETSCAPE ONLY If desired, type **ALIGN=direction**, where *direction* refers to the way a rule should be aligned on the page; either *left, right* or *center*. The ALIGN attribute is only effective if you have made the rule narrower than the document.

5. NETSCAPE ONLY If desired, type **NOSHADE** to create a solid bar, with no shading.

6. Type the final **>** to complete the horizontal rule definition.

LINKS AND ANCHORS

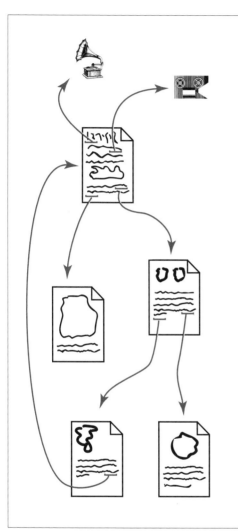

Figure 4-1. *Some of your pages may have links to many other pages. Other pages may have only one link. And still others may have no links at all.*

Creating links

Links are the distinguishing feature of the World Wide Web. They let you skip from one page to another, call up a movie or a recording of Bill playing his sax, and download files with FTP.

To create a link:

1. Type **<A HREF="url.address">** where the *url.address* is the URL of the destination page.

2. Type the clickable text, that is, the text that will be underlined or highlighted in blue, and that when clicked upon will take the user to the URL referenced in step 1.

3. Type **</A>** to complete the definition of the link.

✔ Tips

- Don't use excessive amounts of clickable text. If the clickable text is part of a longer sentence, keep only the key words within the link definition, with the rest of the sentence before and after the less than and greater signs.

- Don't use "Click here" as clickable text. Instead use the key words that already exist in your text to identify the link.

- You may apply text formatting to the clickable text.

Links and Anchors

Using the BASE tag

Generally, relative URLs are constructed according to the current location of the HTML document that contains the URL. If you use relative URLs in your HTML documents (see page 3 for more details), you can use the BASE tag to specify the URL of the current HTML document.

To create a base URL:

1. In the HEAD section of your HTML document (after <HEAD> but before </HEAD>, type **<BASE HREF="**.

2. Type **http://www.site.com/path/ filename.html** where *http:// www.site.com/path/filename.html* indicates the desired URL for the HTML file. All relative URLs contained in the HTML document will be built using this URL as a reference.

3. Type **">** to complete the BASE tag.

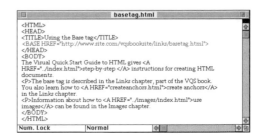

Figure 4-2. *The BASE tag, which goes in the HEAD section of the HTML document, gives the URL of the current file, in this case that of* basetag.html.

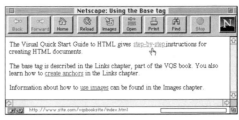

Figure 4-3. *The relative URL,* ../index.html, *combined with the base URL results in the file that is in the directory that is one level higher than the base URL's directory.*

Figure 4-4. *The relative URL,* createanchors.html, *combined with the base URL indicates the file will be in the current directory.*

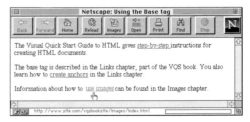

Figure 4-5. *The relative URL,* ../images/index.html, *combined with the base URL indicates the file that is inside the directory* images *which is at the same level as the current directory.*

Figure 4-6. *Only the text within the link definition (in this case the words* Pioneer Valley*) will be clickable.*

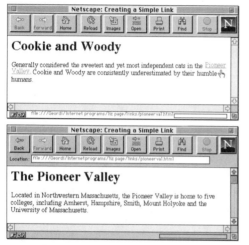

Figure 4-7. *A click on a link (generally shown with underlined or blue text or both) brings you to the associated URL (below).*

Creating a link to another Web page

If you have more than one Web page, you will probably want to create links from one page to the next (and back again). You can also create connections to Web pages designed by other people on other computers. Whenever you create a link to another Web page, you must use the HTTP protocol.

To create a link to another Web page using HTTP:

1. Type **<A HREF="http://www.site. com/homepage.html">** where *www.site.com/homepage.html* is the URL of the Web page. *www.site.com* is the name of the server and *homepage.html* is the file name of the destination page.

2. Type the clickable text, that is, the text that will be underlined or highlighted in blue, and that when clicked upon will take the user to the URL referenced in step 1.

3. Type **</A>** to complete the definition of the link.

✔ Tip

■ You can often create a link to a site's home page without knowing what the name of the home page is by using *http://www.site.com/directory/*. The trailing forward slash tells the browser to search for the default file—usually called *index.html*—in the last directory mentioned, which in this example is, *directory*.

Creating anchors

Generally, a click on a link brings the user to the *top* of the appropriate Web page. If you want to have the user jump to a specific section of the Web page, you have to create an *anchor* and then reference that anchor in the link.

To create an anchor:

1. Place the cursor in the part of the Web page that you wish the user to jump to.

2. Type **<A NAME="anchor name">**, where *anchor name* is the text you will use internally to identify that section of the Web page.

3. Add the words or images that you wish to be referenced.

4. Type **</A>** to complete the definition of the anchor.

✔ Tips

■ You only need to add quotation marks around the anchor name if it is more than one word.

■ In a long document, create an anchor for each section and link it to the corresponding item in the table of contents.

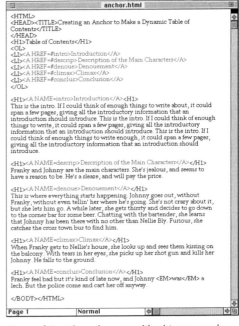

Figure 4-8. *A long document like this one can be greatly helped by a dynamic table of contents. In this example, each section has its own anchor name so that a click on the corresponding item in the table of contents brings the user directly to the section they're interested in. (See Figures 4-9 and 4-10 on page 65.)*

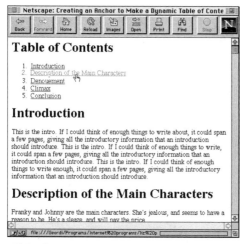

Figure 4-9. *A click in the referenced link brings the user...*

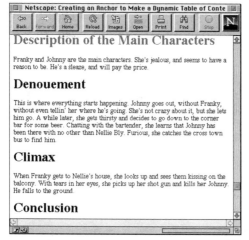

Figure 4-10. *...to the corresponding anchor farther down in the same document (as in this example) or to a specific position in a separate document.*

Linking to a specific anchor

Once you have created an anchor you can define a link so that a user's click will bring them directly to the section of the document that contains the anchor, not just the top of that document.

To create a link to an anchor:

1. Type **<A HREF="#**.

2. Type **anchor name"** where *anchor name* is the NAME of the destination section. (See previous page.)

3. Type the clickable text, that is, the text that will be underlined or highlighted in blue, and that when clicked upon will take the user to the section referenced in step 1.

4. Type **</A>** to complete the definition of the link.

✔ Tips

■ If the anchor is in a separate document, use *<A HREF="url.address #anchor name">* to reference the section. (There should be no space between *url.address* and the # symbol.)

■ Although you obviously can't add anchors to other people's pages, you can take advantage of the ones that they have already created. Save their documents in HTML format to see which anchor names correspond to which sections. (See page 126 for more information on saving HTML code.)

Linking to a specific anchor

Linking to an anonymous FTP site

You can create links to FTP servers directly from your Web page. Many browsers can complete non-Web type connections, while others automatically open an appropriate helper program (like Fetch) if they can't handle the connection directly.

To create a link to an FTP site:

1. Type **<A HREF="ftp://ftp.site.com/ directory/filename">** where *ftp.site.com/directory/filename* is the URL of the destination file available through FTP.

2. Type the clickable text, that is, the text that will be underlined or highlighted in blue, and that when clicked upon will take the user to the URL referenced in step 1.

3. Type **</A>** to complete the definition of the link.

✔ Tips

■ If you don't want to create the link to a specific file, but instead to a particular directory on the FTP site, simply use *ftp://ftp.site.com/directory*. You don't need to use the trailing forward slash. When you don't specify a particular file to download, FTP automatically displays the last directory's contents.

■ A user may have trouble connecting to an anonymous FTP site if they have not filled in their e-mail address in the browser's preferences or settings dialog box.

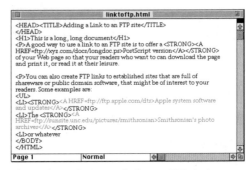

Figure 4-11. *Creating a link to an FTP site is very similar to creating a link to a Web page; just substitute the FTP site address in the link definition.*

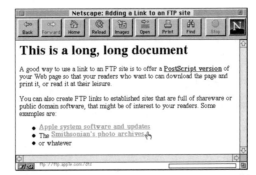

Figure 4-12. *As with links to Web pages, you should incorporate your links to FTP sites right into your text. Here I've used strong formatting to help the links stand out better.*

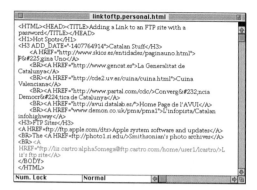

Figure 4-13. *Add the user name and password before the site name in the URL address.*

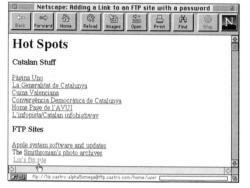

Figure 4-14. *Since you don't want to share the password to your (or anyone else's) account with the rest of the world, only include the user name and password to FTP sites in personal pages on a local computer.*

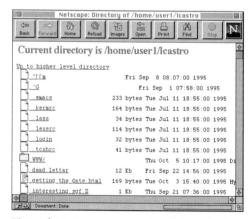

Figure 4-15. *Once you connect to the FTP site, it works the same way as anonymous FTP connections. (Pardon the mess!)*

Linking to an FTP site with a user name and password

Not all FTP sites accept anonymous connections. You may include a link to an FTP site using your user name and password, but since there is no way to hide your password, you should not use this kind of link in a page that is published on the Web for all to see.

To create a link to an FTP site with a user name and password:

1. Type **<A HREF="ftp://yourname: password@ftp.site.com/directory/">** where *yourname* is your user name, *password* is your password and *ftp.site.com/directory/* is the URL of the destination directory available through FTP.

2. Type the clickable text, that is, the text that will be underlined or highlighted in blue, and that when clicked upon will take the user to the URL referenced in step 1.

3. Type **</A>** to complete the definition of the link.

✔ Tips

- Add your favorite FTP sites, complete with passwords, to a personal bookmarks or hotlist page that you keep on your local computer.

- If your browser keeps a record of your trips around the Web, it may keep a record of your password as well.

Linking to Gopher servers

Creating a link to a Gopher server is very similar to creating a link to an FTP site.

To create a link to a Gopher server:

1. Type **<A HREF="gopher://site.edu">** where *site.edu* is the URL of the Gopher server.

2. Type the clickable text, that is, the text that will be underlined or highlighted in blue, and that when clicked upon will take the user to the URL referenced in step 1.

3. Type **</A>** to complete the definition of the link.

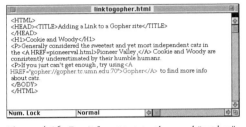

Figure 4-16. *Don't forget to type the word "gopher" twice, once as the protocol and once as part of the domain name.*

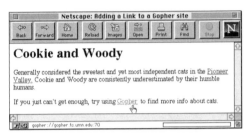

Figure 4-17. *OK, the text here is not particularly brilliant, but the idea is clear: make the link part of your text.*

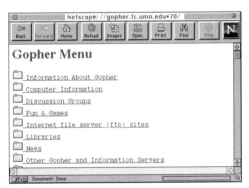

Figure 4-18. *Once the user clicks on your Gopher link they are directly connected to the Gopher site and can perform their search as usual. Other browsers may choose to open a Gopher helper program (like TurboGopher) instead.*

Figure 4-19. *A mailto URL does not use forward slashes; a colon divides the protocol name (mailto) from the recipient's e-mail address.*

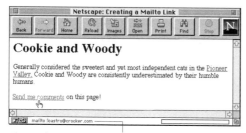

Figure 4-20. *Placing the cursor over the mailto link shows the recipient's e-mail address in the destination area of the browser (below left in the Netscape window as shown here).*

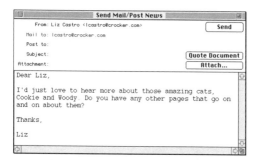

Figure 4-21. *Once the user clicks the mailto link, an e-mail form pops up with the From: and To: boxes automatically filled in. If you respond to your own Web pages, you, too, can write schizophrenic notes like this one.*

Linking to e-mail

Although not all browsers currently support e-mail links, the ones that do make it quite easy for your users to contact you. A link to e-mail is called a *mailto* and is a special link that pops up an automatically addressed e-mail form.

To create a mailto link:

1. Type **<A HREF="mailto:name@ site.com">** where *name@site.com* is the electronic mail address of the person who should receive the mail.

2. Type the clickable text, that is, the text that will be underlined or highlighted, and that when clicked upon will open an e-mail form addressed to the person in step 1.

3. Type **</A>** to complete the definition of the link.

✔ Tip

■ Mailto links are ideal for eliciting comments about your Web page. They ensure that the comments will go to the proper person.

Linking to e-mail

Linking to a newsgroup

You can create a link from your page to an entire newsgroup or to just one article in the newsgroup.

To create a link to a newsgroup:

1. Type **<A HREF="news:newsgroup">** where *newsgroup* is the name of the newsgroup (like *bit.listserv.catala* or *rec.pets.cats*).

2. Type the clickable text, that is, the text that will be underlined or highlighted in blue, and that when clicked upon will take the user to the URL referenced in step 1.

3. Type **</A>** to complete the definition of the link.

To create a link to a single article:

1. Type **<A HREF="news:articlenumb">** where *articlenumb* is the number (as shown in the header) of the individual article.

2. Type the clickable text, that is, the text that will be underlined or highlighted in blue, and that when clicked upon will take the user to the URL referenced in step 1.

3. Type **</A>** to complete the definition of the link.

✔ Tip

■ In NewsWatcher, choose Show Details from the Edit menu to display the Message ID. Then copy it directly to your HTML document.

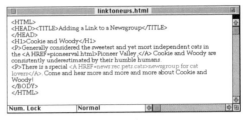

Figure 4-22. *The newsgroup protocol is formatted differently than most others, with a colon and no forward slashes.*

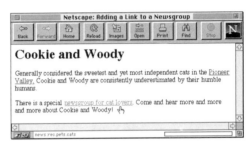

Figure 4-23. *This particular newsgroup is remarkably active, with three hundred messages daily. It's a bit of a struggle to keep up with, even for a cat lover.*

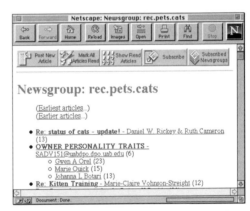

Figure 4-24. *Netscape has an excellent format for displaying Usenet newsgroups, including navigation buttons and a pretty effective threading system.*

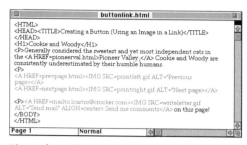

Figure 4-25. *There is no text in the first two button links. The final </A> comes right after the image source information.*

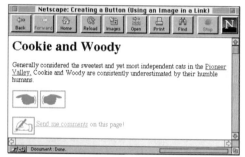

Figure 4-26. *If you do add text to the link, make sure you insert a space between the text and the image (or use Netscape's extensions to space the text, see page 52).*

Figure 4-27. *This is the original* pointright.gif *image. It does not have a border. Borders are automatically added to all clickable images in the browser.*

Creating navigational buttons

In this age of graphical interfaces, people are used to clicking on images and icons to make things happen. Adding an image to a link allows the user to click the image to access the referenced URL. (For more information about how to create and use images, see Chapter 3.)

To create links with buttons:

1. Type **<A HREF="url.address">** where *url.address* identifies the page that the user will jump to when they click the button.

2. Type **<IMG SRC="image.location"** where *image.location* gives the location of the image file on the server.

3. Add other image attributes as desired and then type the final **>**.

4. Type the clickable text, that is, the text that will be underlined or highlighted in blue, that when clicked upon will take the user to the URL referenced in step 1.

5. Type **</A>** to complete the link definition.

✔ Tips

■ If you invert steps 4 and 5, only a click on the *image* will produce the desired jump. A click on the text will do nothing.

■ Use small images.

■ Clickable images are surrounded by a border with the same color as the active links (generally blue).

Dividing an image into clickable regions

A clickable image is like a collection of buttons combined together in one image. A click in one part of the image brings the user to one destination. A click in another area brings the user to a different destination.

There are two important steps to implementing a clickable image: First you must map out the different regions of your image, and second you must create a script that defines which destinations correspond to which areas of the image.

To divide an image into regions:

1. Create a GIF image, consulting Chapter 3 as necessary.

2. Open the GIF image in Photoshop, or other image editing program.

3. Choose Show Info in the Palettes submenu in the Window menu.

4. Point the cursor over the region you wish to define. Using the Info window, jot down the necessary *x* and *y* coordinates, according to the table (**Figure 4-29**).

5. Repeat step 4 for each region.

✔ Tip

■ See page 155 for information on a few tools that can help you divide your image into clickable regions.

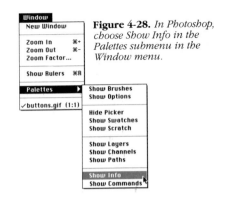

Figure 4-28. *In Photoshop, choose Show Info in the Palettes submenu in the Window menu.*

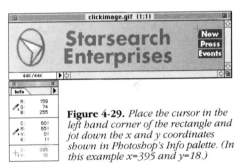

Figure 4-29. *Place the cursor in the left hand corner of the rectangle and jot down the x and y coordinates shown in Photoshop's Info palette. (In this example x=395 and y=18.)*

Figure 4-30. *If you use an NCSA HTTPd server, your image map should look like this.*

Figure 4-31. *In an image map for a CERN server, parentheses surround each set of coordinates.*

Creating an image map

To create an image map that links the regions of an image with a series of URLs, you must list each kind of region, the x and y coordinates that define the region, and the corresponding URL that should be accessed when the user clicks in the region.

To create an image map:

1. Open a text editor or word processor.

2. On the first line, type **#Image map for image.gif** where *image.gif* is the name of the image that contains the regions to be defined, and then press the **Return** key. This line is optional— the # denotes a comment that is not used by the server—but it helps keep everything straight.

3. Type **default url.default** and then press the **Return** key where *url.default* is the page that the browser should show if the user clicks in an undefined region. By including the default line, you guarantee that any click on any area of the image will have some effect, thus minimizing user frustration. (Also, see tip.)

4. Type **shape**, where *shape* is the type of region. For NCSA HTTPd servers, use *circle* for a circle, *rect* for rectangles and squares, *poly* for an irregular shape with up to 100 sides, and *point* for an individual point. For CERN servers, use *circle* for a circle, *polygon* for a polygon and *rectangle* for a rectangle. CERN servers do not support points. (See Table 4-32 on page 74.)

5. Press the **Tab** or Space key.

Creating an image map

6. Type **url.address** where *url.address* is the location of the page that the user should jump to when they click in this region.

7. Press the **Tab** or Space key.

8. For NCSA HTTPd servers, type **x,y** for each point to be defined in the region, where *x* is the x coordinate and *y* is the y coordinate of the given point. Separate each set of points with a space.

For CERN servers, type **(x,y)** for each point to be defined in the region, where x is the x coordinate and y is the y coordinate of the given point. For circles, type **(x,y) r** where *r* is the radius of the circle. Separate each set of points with a space.

9. Press the **Return** key.

10. Repeat steps 4-9 for each region you wish to define.

11. Save the document as text only.

✔ **Tip**

■ You should define more than one point, or none at all. A click is considered to be *on* a point when it is closest to that point's coordinates (and outside contained regions). Therefore, if you have defined only one point, any click will be the "closest". (When you have defined one or more points, there is no reason to use the default line—once you have a point, no click can be outside a clickable region.)

For NCSA HTTPd server	
Shape	*Get x, y of...*
circle	center, edgepoint
point	point
polygon	each point that defines the perimeter of the polygon
rectangle	the top left and bottom right corners

For CERN server	
Shape	*Get x, y of...*
circle	edgepoint (and get radius)
polygon	each point that defines the perimeter of the polygon
rectangle	the top left and bottom right corners

Table 4-32. *Depending on the kind of server you use, you need to gather slightly different information about the shapes in your clickable image.*

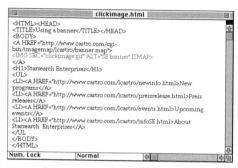

Figure 4-33. *Notice how the text-based alternative pointers below the image point to the same URLs as the buttons in the clickable image. This gives equal opportunity to your users that can't see the images.*

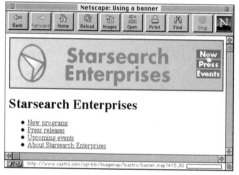

Figure 4-34. *In Netscape, when your user points at a part of a clickable image, the cursor changes into a hand and the corresponding URL shows in the bottom part of the window.*

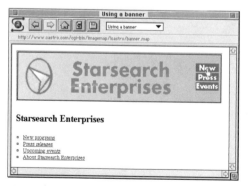

Figure 4-35. *In Mosaic, the cursor changes to a hand when placed over a clickable image, but the status line (between the buttons and the Web page) does not show the particular coordinates.*

Using an image map

To use an image map, you have to have the *imagemap* program on your NCSA HTTPd server or *htimage* on your CERN server. The program should be located in the cgi-bin directory. Ask your server administrator for help, if necessary.

To use an image map:

1. In your HTML document type **<A HREF="http://www.yoursite.com/cgi-bin/imagemap**, where *imagemap* is the name of the program that interprets your set of coordinates.

2. Type **/path/mapname"** (adding no spaces after step 1) which should indicate the path to the map you have created, relative to the location of the imagemap program on the server.

3. Type the final **>** of the first part of the link definition.

4. Type **<IMG SRC="clickimage.gif"** where *clickimage.gif* is the image that you want your readers to click.

5. Type **ISMAP** to indicate that the image is a clickable image.

6. Add any other image attributes as desired and then type the final **>**.

7. Type the clickable text that should appear next to the image, if any.

8. Type **</A>** to complete the link definition.

✔ Tip

■ Provide alternative text (or a separate text-based menu) for users who may not see the image due to their browser or graphics capabilities.

LISTS

The HTML specifications contain special codes for creating lists of items. You can create plain, numbered or bulleted lists, as well as lists of definitions. You can also nest one kind of list inside another. In the sometimes sketchy shorthand of the Internet, lists come in very handy.

All lists are formed by a principal code to specify what sort of list you want to create (DL for definition list, OL for ordered list, etc.) and a secondary code to specify what sort of items you want to create (DT for definition term, LI for list item, etc.).

Creating ordered lists

The ordered list is perfect for explaining step-by-step instructions for how to complete a particular task or for creating an outline (complete with links to corresponding sections, if desired) of a larger document. You may create an ordered list anywhere in the BODY section of your HTML document.

To create ordered lists:

1. Type the title of the ordered list.

2. Type **<OL**.

3. 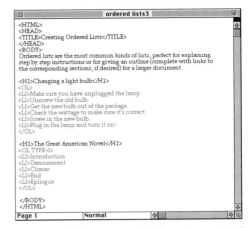 If desired, type **TYPE=X**, where *X* represents the symbols that should be used in the ordered list: *A* for capital letters, *a* for small letters, *I* for capital roman numerals, *i* for small roman numerals and *1* for numbers, which is the default.

4. If desired, type **START=n**, where *n* represents the base value for the this and subsequent list items. The START value is always numeric and is converted automatically, according to the TYPE value.

5. Type **>** to finish the ordered list definition. Any text entered after the OL marker and before the first LI marker will appear with the same indentation as the first item in the list, but without a number.

6. Type **<LI**.

7. If desired, type **TYPE=X**, where *X* represents the symbols that should be used for this and subsequent line items. Changing the TYPE here overrides the value chosen in step 3.

Figure 5-1. *There is some talk of creating a special header for lists in HTML 3, but for now you can just use a regular header.*

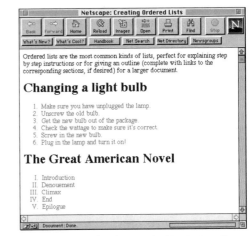

Figure 5-2. *The first list uses the TYPE=1 attribute to create a numbered list. The second list uses the TYPE=I to create a list headed by capital roman numerals.*

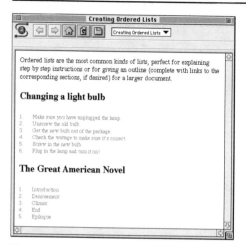

Figure 5-3. *Mosaic ignores Netscape's extensions and displays both lists with regular numbers and its standard formatting.*

8. If desired, type **VALUE=n**, where *n* represents the initial value for this and subsequent line items. The VALUE is always specified numerically and is converted automatically to the type of symbol specified by the TYPE value. The VALUE attribute overrides the START value chosen in step 4.

9. Type the final **>** to complete the list item definition.

10. Type the text to be included in the line item.

11. Repeat steps 6 to 10 for each new line item.

12. Type **</OL>** to complete the ordered list.

✔ **Tips**

■ Keep the text in your list items short. If you have more than a few lines of text in each item, you may have better luck using headers (H1, H2, etc.) and paragraphs (P).

■ Inserting a line break (BR) in a list item breaks the text to the next line, but maintains the same indenting.

■ Text placed after the OL marker appears indented by the same amount as the following line item, but without a number or letter.

■ You may create one type of list inside another. (See page 83 for details.)

Creating unordered lists

Unordered lists are probably the most widely used lists on the Web. Use them to list any series of items that have no particular order, such as hot web sites or names.

To create unordered lists:

1. Type the introductory text for the unordered list, if desired.

2. Type **<UL**.

3. If desired, type **TYPE=shape**, where *shape* represents the kind of bullet that should be used with each list item. You may choose *disc* for a solid round bullet (the default for first level lists), *round* for an empty round bullet (the default for second level lists), or *square* for square bullets (the default for third level lists).

4. Type **>** to finish the unordered list definition. Any text entered after the UL marker and before the first LI marker will appear with the same indentation as the first item in the list, but without a bullet.

5. Type **<LI**.

6. Type **TYPE=shape**, where *shape* represents the kind of bullet (*disc*, *round*, or *square*) that should be used in this line item. You only need to specify the shape here if it differs from the one you've chosen in step 3.

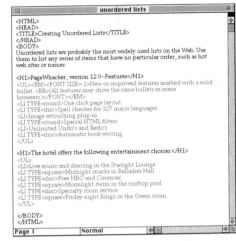

Figure 5-4. *The bullets on the first level are round and solid, by default, so it's not necessary to specify the TYPE unless you wish to select a different shape.*

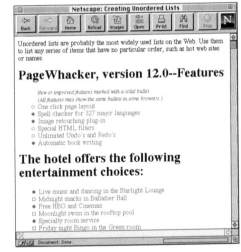

Figure 5-5. *You can use different bullet styles to distinguish among the entries as in the first example, or to add visual interest as in the second example.*

Creating unordered lists

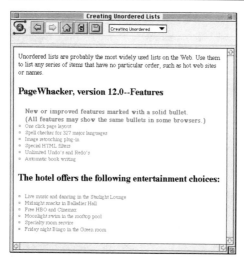

Figure 5-6. *Beware that many browsers, like Mosaic, for example, do not support different shaped bullets. Either avoid giving special meaning to shaped bullets or add a text clarification.*

7. Type **>** to finish the list item definition.

8. Type the text to be included in the line item.

9. Repeat steps 5 to 9 for each line item.

10. Type **</UL>** to complete the unordered list.

✔ Tips

■ Keep the text in your list items short. If you have more than a couple of lines of text in each item, you may have better luck using headers (H1, H2, etc.) and paragraphs (P).

■ Inserting a line break (BR) in a line item breaks the text to the next line, but maintains the same indenting.

■ Text placed after the UL marker appears indented by the same amount as the following line item, but without a bullet.

■ The TYPE marker in a list item overrides the TYPE marker used in the unordered list definition and affects the current list item as well as any subsequent list items.

■ You may create one type of list inside another. (See page 83 for details.)

Creating definition lists

HTML provides a special marker for creating definition lists. This type of list is particularly suited to glossaries but works well with any list that pairs a word or phrase with a longer description. Imagine for example a list of types of mushrooms, each followed by the main characteristics that separate the gourmet from the deadly.

To create definition lists:

1. Type the introductory text for the definition list.

2. Type **<DL>**. You may enter text after the **DL** marker. It will appear on its own line, aligned to the left margin.

3. Type **<DT>**.

4. Type the word or short phrase that will be defined or explained, including any logical or physical formatting desired.

5. Type **<DD>**.

6. Type the definition of the term entered in step 4. Browsers generally indent definitions on a new line below your definition term.

7. Repeat steps 3 to 6 for each pair of terms and definitions.

8. Type **</DL>** to complete the list of definitions.

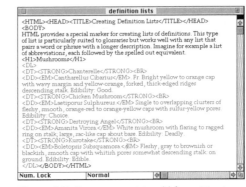

Figure 5-7. *You may want to add formatting to your definition term to help it stand out.*

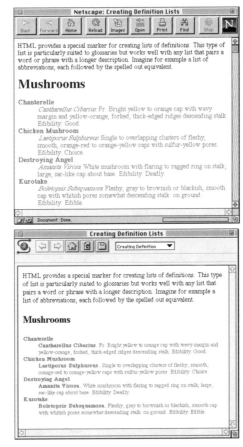

Figure 5-8. *Definition lists don't change their appearance much from browser to browser. This is NCSA Mosaic and the middle screen is Netscape.*

Creating definition lists

```
nested lists

<HTML>
<HEAD>
<TITLE>Creating Nested Lists</TITLE>
</HEAD>
<BODY>
Nested lists are ideal for outlines, but don't feel limited. You can nest any
list inside any other list. Just make sure each list has its own beginning and
ending markers.

<H1>The Great American Novel</H1>
<OL TYPE=I>
<LI>Introduction
    <OL TYPE=A>
    <LI>Boy's childhood
    <LI>Girl's childhood
    </OL>
<LI>Denouement
    <OL TYPE=A>
    <LI>Boy meets Girl
    <LI>Boy and Girl fall in love
    <LI>Boy and Girl have fight
    </OL>
<LI>Climax
    <OL TYPE=A>
    <LI>Boy gives Girl ultimatum
        <OL TYPE=I>
        <LI>Girl can't believe her ears
        <LI>Boy is indignant at Girl's indignance
        </OL>
    <LI>Girl tells Boy to get lost
    </OL>
<LI>End
<LI>Epilogue
</OL>

</BODY>
</HTML>

Page 1                    Normal
```

Figure 5-9. *Browsers automatically indent nested lists, but if you use tabs to indent them in your HTML document, it will be much easier to read.*

```
Netscape: Creating Nested Lists

Back  Forward  Home  Reload  Images  Open  Print  Find  Stop    N
What's New?  What's Cool?  Handbook  Net Search  Net Directory  Newsgroups

Nested lists are ideal for outlines, but don't feel limited. You can nest any list
inside any other list. Just make sure each list has its own beginning and ending
markers.
```

The Great American Novel

```
I. Introduction
    A. Boy's childhood
    B. Girl's childhood
II. Denouement
    A. Boy meets Girl
    B. Boy and Girl fall in love
    C. Boy and Girl have fight
III. Climax
    A. Boy gives Girl ultimatum
        1. Girl can't believe her ears
        2. Boy is indignant at Girl's indignance
    B. Girl tells Boy to get lost
IV. End
V. Epilogue

Document: Done.
```

Figure 5-10. *Netscape allows you, the programmer, to choose the type of numbering for each level of your outline. Most other browsers do not.*

Creating nested lists

You may insert one type of list into another. This is particularly useful with an outline rendered with ordered lists, where you may want several levels of items.

To create nested lists:

1. Create your first list.

2. Place the cursor inside your first list where you want your nested list to appear.

3. Create your nested list in the same way you created the regular list.

4. Continue with the principal list.

✔ Tips

■ If you use tabs to indent the nested list in your HTML document, it will be easier to keep track of. Nested lists are automatically indented by browsers.

■ Nested ordered lists automatically start at one unless you specify a new value with the START marker.

■ The correct nesting order for TYPE markers, according to *The Chicago Manual of Style* is I, A, 1, a, 1.

■ By default, the first level of an unordered list will have solid round bullets, the next will have empty round bullets and the last will have square bullets. Use the TYPE tag to specify the type of bullet you want. (See page 80.)

TABLES

There is nothing like a table for presenting complicated information in a simple way. Your user sees what you're getting at right away and everyone goes home happy. Too bad tables are so hard to set up. Don't be scared off, though; the result is worth the effort.

If tables really make you miserable, of course, you can cheat. Try the shortcut described on page 132 if you use Microsoft Word, or use the rtftohtml filter described on page 153.

If you are worried about users who use a browser that doesn't understand tables, you might consider creating hand spaced tables with preformatted text. (See page 21.) Tables made with preformatted text can be read by *any* browser.

A simple table

There are many kinds of tables, and even many kinds of simple tables. Here we will create a table with two columns and three rows, using the first column to contain the headers and the second column to contain the data.

To create a simple table:

1. Type **<TABLE>**.

2. Type **<TR>** to define the beginning of the first row. We will add two elements to the first row, a header cell and a regular cell. If desired, press Return and Tab to visually distinguish the row elements.

3. Create a header cell in the first row by typing **<TH>**.

4. Type the contents of the first header cell.

5. Type **</TH>** to complete the definition of the first cell header.

6. Create a regular cell after the header cell in the first row by typing **<TD>**.

7. Type the contents of the regular cell.

8. Complete the definition of the regular cell by typing **</TD>**.

9. Complete the definition of the row by typing **</TR>**.

10. Repeat steps 3-9 for each row. In this example, there are two more rows, each containing a header cell and a regular cell.

11. To finish the table, type **</TABLE>**.

Figure 6-1. *The only difference between the two HTML documents above is the addition of returns and tabs to visually separate the rows and row elements to help keep things straight while constructing the table. Since browsers ignore all extra spacing, both documents create the exact same Web page. (See Figures 6-2 and 6-3 below.)*

Figure 6-2. *It seems rather a lot of work for a simple table like this. Notice how Netscape formats the header cells in boldface and centers them while it leaves regular cells in plain text and left aligned.*

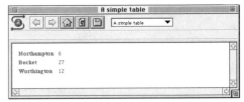

Figure 6-3. *Mosaic formats the header cells in boldface but aligns them to the left. Regular cells are in plain text and left aligned, by default.*

A simple table

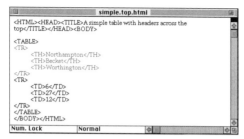

Figure 6-4. *In the first row, you define all the headers. In the second row, you define all the regular cells.*

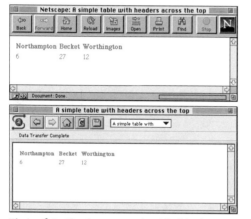

Figure 6-5. *Clearly, very simple tables like these may be better off expressed in lists. However, as you will see in the following pages, there are many ways to tweak your tables to make them beautiful—and more effective.*

Putting headers across the top of the table

On the previous page, in our simple table, we placed the headers along one side of the table. To have the headers appear along the top of the table, you have to define the cells in a slightly different order.

To create a table with headers across the top:

1. Type **<TABLE>**.

2. Type **<TR>** to define the beginning of the first row. If desired, press Return and Tab to visually distinguish the table elements.

3. Create the first header cell in the first row by typing **<TH>**.

4. Type the contents of the first header cell.

5. Type **</TH>** to complete the definition of the cell header.

6. Repeat steps 3–5 for each header cell.

7. Type **</TR>** to complete the row.

8. Type **<TR>** to begin the second row.

9. Type **<TD>** to define the first regular cell in the second row.

10. Type the cell data.

11. Type **</TD>** to complete the definition of the regular cell.

12. Repeat steps 9–11 for each regular cell.

13. Type **</TR>** to finish the row.

14. To finish the table, type **</TABLE>**.

Putting headers across the top

Putting headers on top *and* left

The objective of a table is to present complicated data in a clear way. Often you will need headers across the top of the table *and* down the left side to identify the data being discussed.

To create a table with headers on top and down the left side:

1. Type **<TABLE>**.

2. Type **<TR>** to define the beginning of the first row. If desired, press Return and Tab to visually distinguish the table elements.

3. Create the empty cell in the top left corner by typing **<TD>
</TD>**.

4. Create a header cell by typing **<TH>cell contents</TH>**, where *cell contents* is the data that the cell should contain.

5. Repeat step 4 for each header cell in the first row.

6. Type **</TR>** to finish the row.

7. Type **<TR>** to begin the second row.

8. To define the first header on the left side, type **<TH>cell contents</TH>**.

9. Type **<TD>cell contents</TD>** to create a regular cell after the header cell in the second row.

10. Repeat step 9 for each remaining regular cell in the row.

11. Type **</TR>** to finish the row.

12. Repeat steps 7-11 for each remaining row.

13. To finish the table, type **</TABLE>**.

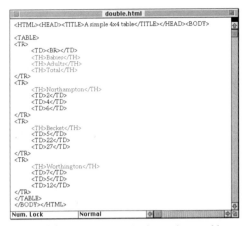

Figure 6-6. *For a four row by four column table, notice that there are four sets of TR tags with four elements in each set. Once you have defined the first set, copy and paste (and edit) to create the rest.*

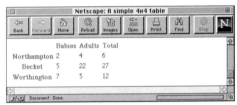

Figure 6-7. *Netscape's tables look impressively bad without borders. (You'll add one on page 89.)*

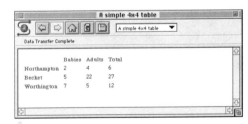

Figure 6-8. *Mosaic, on the other hand, uses simple formatting that helps you read the data.*

Figure 6-9. *The BORDER attribute is added to the initial TABLE tag.*

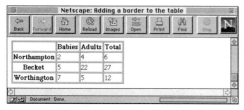

Figure 6-10. *Netscape creates a shaded border (using the background color) around each individual cell and around the table itself.*

Figure 6-11. *Mosaic uses relief shading to set tables apart. If the user has chosen a very light colored background, the table border is much less effective.*

Figure 6-12. *Adding a numeric value to the BORDER tag has no effect (good or bad) on Mosaic.*

Adding a border

Giving your table a border helps separate it from the rest of the text.

To create a border:

1. Inside the initial TABLE tag, type **BORDER**.

2. If desired, type **=n**, where *n* is the thickness in pixels of the border (**Figures 6-12 and 6-13**).

✔ Tips

■ The width value has no affect whatsoever on the Mosaic browser. Your users with Netscape will see fatter borders while your Mosaic users will see the tables as usual.

■ Both browsers shade the border based on the background color, which means that the border loses effectiveness if either you or the user has chosen a light colored background

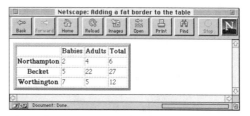

Figure 6-13. *In Netscape, the shading makes a table jump out of the page. There is presently no way to change the shading effect—unfortunately. This table has a border 5 pixels wide.*

89

Adding a caption

The CAPTION tag lets you attach a descriptive title to your table.

To create a caption:

1. After the initial <TABLE> tag, but not inside any row or cell tags, type **<CAPTION**.

2. ▦ By default, the caption will appear above the table. However, if desired, type **ALIGN=bottom** to place the caption below the table **(Figures 6-17 and 6-18)**.

3. Type the final **>**.

4. Type the caption for the table: **Bear Sightings in Western Massachusetts**.

5. Type **</CAPTION>**.

✔ Tip

■ The ALIGN option *top* also exists, but there isn't much point in using it, since the default already places the caption at the top of the table.

Figure 6-14. *A good place to put your caption is right under the TABLE tag.*

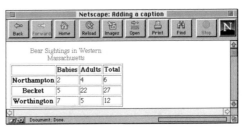

Figure 6-15. *Netscape centers captions automatically and divides the lines to fit the table width.*

Figure 6-16. *Mosaic aligns captions to the left and formats them in boldface.*

Figure 6-17. *Add the ALIGN=bottom attribute inside your CAPTION tag to place the caption below your table.*

Figure 6-18. *Presently, only Netscape can show captions below a table.*

Figure 6-19. *Adding cell spacing increases the distance between each cell, without making the individual cells bigger.*

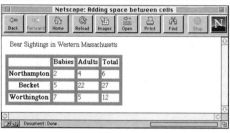

Figure 6-20. *Adding cell padding makes the cells larger, with more space around the contents.*

Spacing and padding the cells

Our table is a little squished, to be frank. Making the cells a bit larger helps make the information easier to read.

NETSCAPE ONLY Cell spacing adds space between cells, making the table bigger without changing the size of individual cells.

To add cell spacing:

1. Within the initial TABLE tag, type **CELLSPACING=n**, where *n* is the number of pixels desired between each cell. (The attribute *cellspacing* is one word.)

The default value for cell spacing is 2 pixels.

NETSCAPE ONLY Cell padding adds space around the contents of a cell, in effect, pushing the walls of the cell outward.

To add cell padding:

1. Within the initial TABLE tag, type **CELLPADDING=n**, where *n* is the number of pixels desired between the contents and the walls of the cell. (The attribute *cellpadding* is one word.) The default value for cell padding is 1 pixel.

✔ Tip

■ The alignment options (see page 96) consider the cell padding as the actual cell limits, and thus, may give unexpected results.

Changing the width and height of the table

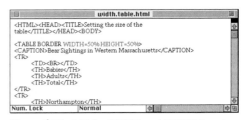

Figure 6-21. *Add the WIDTH and HEIGHT tags to your initial TABLE marker.*

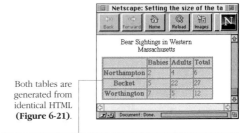

You can use the WIDTH and HEIGHT attributes to resize the whole table, or to define the dimensions of particular cells.

To set the table size:

1. Within the initial TABLE tag, type **WIDTH=x HEIGHT=y**, where *x* and *y* are either absolute values in pixels for the height and width of the table or percentages that indicate how big the table should be with respect to the full window size.

✔ Tips

■ Presently Netscape is the only browser that recognizes the WIDTH and HEIGHT tags. However, the WIDTH tag is part of HTML 3, so future versions of other browsers should incorporate it—some day.

■ You can center a table that is smaller than the total width of the window with the CENTER tag. (See page 19.)

Both tables are generated from identical HTML **(Figure 6-21)**.

Figure 6-22. *If you use a percentage for HEIGHT and WIDTH, the size of the table changes as your user adjusts the size of the window— although it will never get too small to hold the table's contents.*

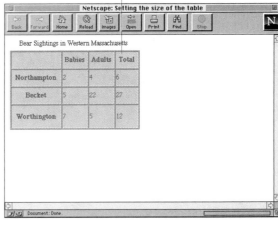

Figure 6-23. *Specify the dimensions of your cell by using the HEIGHT and WIDTH tags inside the cell definition tag (in this case, TH).*

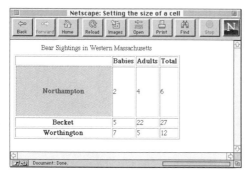

Figure 6-24. *I have had varying results with WIDTH and HEIGHT when used on cells. To tell the truth, I have a feeling they are more trouble than they are worth.*

Figure 6-25. *Add lots of spacing attributes but if your users use Mosaic...*

Figure 6-26. *...the table looks exactly like it did before the additions. (See Figure 6-16 on page 90). If you are counting on the results you get in Netscape with spacing tags, beware. Mosaic does not recognize them (yet).*

Changing the width and height of individual cells

 Netscape's extensions allow you to change the height and width of individual cells.

To change the size of individual cells:

1. Place the cursor inside the cell tag (either TH or TD).

2. Type **WIDTH=x HEIGHT=y**, where *x* and *y* are either absolute values in pixels for the height and width of the cell or percentages that indicate how big the cell should be with respect to the full table size.

✔ Tip

■ Changing one cell's size can affect the size of the entire row or column. You can use this fact to your advantage: you only need to adjust the width of the cells in the first row and the height of the cells in the first column (which is the first cell in each row definition).

Spanning a cell across two or more columns

If you have a lot of information you wish to convey with a table, you can divide a table header into several categories by having it span several columns, and adding more specific headers in the row below.

To span a cell across two columns:

1. When you get to the point in which you need to define the cell that spans more than one column, *either* type **<TH** *or* type **<TD**, depending on whether the cell should be a header cell or a regular cell, respectively.

2. Type **COLSPAN=n>**, where *n* equals the number of columns the cell should span.

3. Type the cell's contents.

4. Type **</TH>** or **</TD>**, to match the tag you used in step 2.

5. Complete the rest of the table. If you create a cell that spans 2 columns, you will need to define one less cell in that row. If you create a cell that spans 3 columns, you will define two less cells for the row.

✔ Tip

■ Writing a table's HTML from scratch is, shall we say, challenging. Try sketching it out on paper first, as described on page 99, to get a handle on which information goes in which row and column. Or you can cheat and use the tip on page 132 or the filter described on page 153.

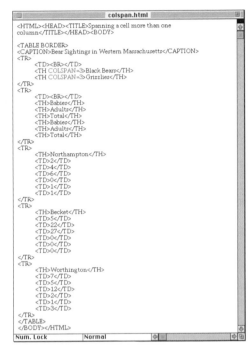

Figure 6-27. *In each row there are seven column positions defined. In the first row there is 1 empty cell and two headers of 3 columns each (1+3+3=7). In the following rows, there is one empty or header cell and six individual cells (1+6=7).*

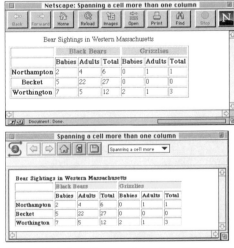

Figure 6-28. *Both Netscape (above) and Mosaic support the COLSPAN tag. (No, there aren't really Grizzly Bears in Western Massachusetts.)*

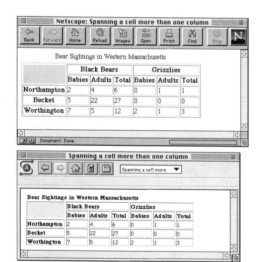

```
rowspan.html
<HTML><HEAD><TITLE>Spanning a cell more than one
row</TITLE></HEAD><BODY>

<TABLE BORDER>
<CAPTION>Bear Sightings in Western Massachusetts</CAPTION>
<TR>
        <TD ROWSPAN=2><BR></TD>
        <TH COLSPAN=3>Black Bears</TH>
        <TH COLSPAN=3>Grizzlies</TH>
</TR>
<TR>
        <TH>Babies</TH>
        <TH>Adults</TH>
        <TH>Total</TH>
        <TH>Babies</TH>
        <TH>Adults</TH>
        <TH>Total</TH>
</TR>
<TR>
        <TH>Northampton</TH>
        <TD>2</TD>
        <TD>4</TD>
        <TD>6</TD>
        <TD>0</TD>
        <TD>1</TD>
        <TD>1</TD>
</TR>
Num. Lock          Normal
```

Figure 6-29. *There are just two differences between this document and the one on the preceding page—besides the fact that I haven't shown the end of the HTML document here. (See Figure 6-27.) First, the blank cell in the first row now spans two rows. Second, because the blank cell spans two rows, the first cell in the second row is already defined, and the original code is thus eliminated from the HTML.*

Figure 6-30. *Now that the empty cell spans two rows, the ugly line that separated the two rows disappears and the table looks much better.*

Spanning a cell across two or more rows

Creating a cell that spans more than one row is essentially identical to spanning more than one column—just from another angle. It is ideal for dividing the headers on the left side of the table into subcategories.

To span a cell across two rows:

1. When you get to the point in which you need to define the cell that spans more than one column, *either* type **<TH** *or* type **<TD**, depending on whether the cell should be a header cell or a regular cell, respectively.

2. Type **ROWSPAN=n>**, where *n* equals the number of rows the cell should span.

3. Type the cell's contents.

4. Type **</TH>** or **</TD>**, to match the tag you used in step 2.

5. Complete the rest of the table. If you define a cell with a rowspan of 2, you will not need to define the cell in the next row. If you define a cell with a rowspan of 3, you will not need to define the cell in the next two rows.

Aligning a cell's contents

Each browser shows the contents of the cells in a table in its own way, by default, which may or may not be how you think the data looks best. To gain a little more control over the alignment of a cell's contents, use the ALIGN (in both Netscape and Mosaic) and VALIGN (just Netscape) tags.

To align a cell's contents horizontally:

1. Place the cursor in the initial tag for the cell, after <TD or <TH but before the final >.

2. Type **ALIGN=direction**, where *direction* is either left, center or right.

✓ Tips

■ Browsers have special algorithms to decide how to view your tables, according to the amount of data in the cell, the size of the window, and (sometimes it seems like) the mood of the browser at that moment. You may need to use the WIDTH and HEIGHT tags to adjust the cell size manually to get the full affect of cell alignment. (See pages 92-93.)

■ If you have added cell padding to a cell's definition, the contents will be aligned *inside* the cell padding, as if the cell padding defined the actual limits of the cell.

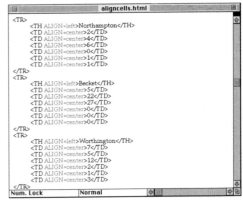

Figure 6-31. *In the same table we've been working with for the last few pages, I've aligned the left hand headers (the city names) to the left, and centered the numerical data.*

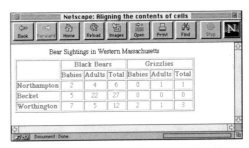

Figure 6-32. *The result is a clearer, more legible table.*

Aligning a cell's contents

```
alignall.html
<HTML><HEAD><TITLE>All the Alignment
Options</TITLE></HEAD><BODY>

<TABLE BORDER>
<CAPTION>Aligning every which way</CAPTION>
<TR>
     <TD COLSPAN=2 ROWSPAN=2><BR></TD>
     <TH COLSPAN=3>HORIZONTAL</TH>
</TR>
<TR>
     <TH>Left</TH>
     <TH>Center</TH>
     <TH>Right</TH>
</TR>
<TR>
     <TH ROWSPAN=4><IMG SRC="vertical.gif"</TH>
     <TH>Top</TH>
     <TD VALIGN=top ALIGN=left WIDTH=110 HEIGHT=80><IMG
SRC="arrows.gif" ALIGN=bottom>Top Left</TD>
     <TD VALIGN=top ALIGN=center WIDTH=110 HEIGHT=80>Top
Center</TD>
     <TD VALIGN=top ALIGN=right WIDTH=110 HEIGHT=80>Top
Right</TD>
</TR>
<TR>
     <TH>Middle</TH>
     <TD VALIGN=middle ALIGN=left WIDTH=110 HEIGHT=80>Middle
Left</TD>
     <TD VALIGN=middle ALIGN=center>Middle Center</TD>
     <TD VALIGN=middle ALIGN=right>Middle Right</TD>
</TR>
<TR>
     <TH>Bottom</TH>
     <TD VALIGN=bottom ALIGN=left WIDTH=110 HEIGHT=80>Bottom
Left</TD>
     <TD VALIGN=bottom ALIGN=center>Bottom Center</TD>
     <TD VALIGN=bottom ALIGN=right>Bottom Right</TD>
</TR>
<TR>
     <TH>Baseline</TH>
     <TD VALIGN=baseline ALIGN=left WIDTH=110 HEIGHT=80><IMG
SRC="arrows.gif" ALIGN=bottom>Baseline Left</TD>
     <TD VALIGN=baseline ALIGN=center>Baseline Center</TD>
     <TD VALIGN=baseline ALIGN=right>Baseline Right</TD>
</TR>
</TABLE>
</BODY></HTML>
Num. Lock          Normal
```

Figure 6-33. *I had to add the WIDTH and HEIGHT tags to make the cells big enough to show the difference between the alignments. If there is no extra space, there is not much difference between left and right aligned, for example.*

 You can use the VALIGN attribute to align the cell's contents vertically.

To align a cell's contents vertically:

1. Place the cursor in the initial tag for the cell, after <TD or <TH but before the final >.

2. Type **VALIGN=direction**, where *direction* is either top, middle, bottom or baseline.

The first three options align every element (including graphics) to the extreme top, middle or bottom of the cell.

The baseline option aligns the contents of each cell according to the baseline of the first line of text in each cell, which may be affected by how the graphics, if any, are aligned **(Figure 6-34)**.

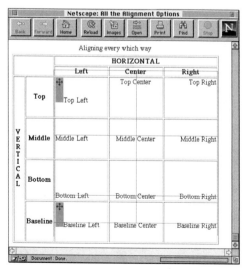

Figure 6-34. *Although the* Top Left *and* Baseline Left *boxes look identical, they are not. The colored lines indicate where the cell content's are aligned. (What's the trick to showing VERTICAL from top to bottom? I used a graphic.)*

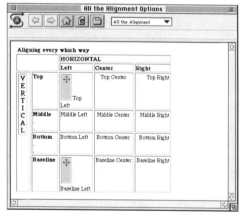

Figure 6-35. *Mosaic neither recognizes the VALIGN tag, nor the HEIGHT and WIDTH tags, making the table much less effective. To make the Middle and Bottom rows taller, I added line breaks and periods before viewing the document in Mosaic.*

Controlling line breaks in a cell

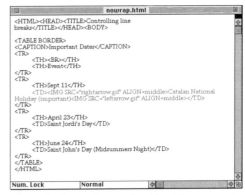

**NETSCAPE ONLY** Unless you specify otherwise, browsers will divide the lines of text in a cell as it decides on the height and width of each column and row. The NOWRAP attribute lets you keep all the text in a cell on one line.

Figure 6-36. *Here's a simple table with two columns and four rows. A browser will stretch out a row as wide as it can before shifting some elements to the next line.*

To keep text in a cell on one single line:

1. Place the cursor in the initial tag for the cell, after <TD or <TH but before the final >.

2. Type **NOWRAP**.

✔ Tips

■ Netscape will make the cell—and the table that contains it—as wide as it needs to accommodate the single line of text. Even if it looks really ugly.

■ You can use regular line breaks (BR) between words to mark where you *do* want the text to break.

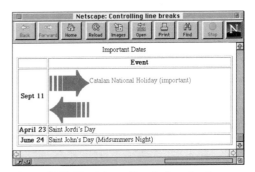

Figure 6-37. *Notwithstanding the fact that these arrows are a little strident for this small table, the arrows should at least be on the same line, aligned with the text.*

Figure 6-38. *This small excerpt of the nowrap.html document shows the only change: the addition of NOWRAP to the first regular cell on the second row.*

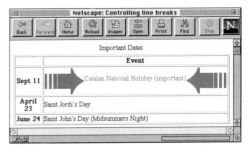

Figure 6-39. *As the arrows were shoehorned into the right column, the left column was compacted just enough to force "April 23" onto two lines. A NOWRAP in the corresponding cell definition will solve the problem.*

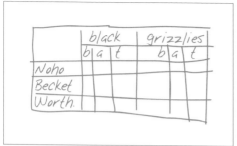

Figure 6-40. *First, draw out your table as simply as possible, including all your headers, but no data.*

Figure 6-41. *To separate the table into rows and columns, draw a line from one end to another (either top to bottom or right to left) everywhere there is a division in the table. In this table, we find five rows and seven columns.*

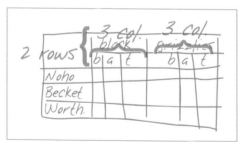

Figure 6-42. *Mark the cells that span more than one column or row. In this example, there is the top left blank row that spans 2 rows (but just 1 column), and the "black" and "grizzlies" headers that span 3 columns each (but just one row). Every other cell spans exactly one column and one row.*

Mapping out a table

Setting up complicated tables in HTML can be really confusing. All you need are a couple of column spans to throw the whole thing off. The trick is to draw a map of your table before you start.

To map out your table:

1. Sketch your table quickly on a piece of paper (yes, with a pen) **(Figure 6-40)**.

2. Divide the table into rows and columns. Number each row and column **(Figure 6-41)**.

3. Mark the cells that will span more than one column or row **(Figure 6-42)**.

4. Count the number of cells in each row (1 point for single cells, 2 points for cells that span two columns, 3 for cells that span three columns, etc.). There should be as many cell definitions in each row as there are columns in the table. (See step 2.)

5. Once you have your table straight on paper, write the HTML code, row by row.

FORMS

One of the most powerful parts of the Web page is the form. In conjunction with *CGI scripts,* forms let you collect information from the user and store it for later use.

In this chapter, you will first learn how to construct forms with regular HTML tags. It is extremely straightforward and is analogous to creating any other part of the Web page.

The most unusual part of a form element is the concept of name/value pairs. Basically, when the information is sent to the server, it is sent in two parts: first an identifier, or name, and then the actual data. For example, in a text box with a name like *Lastname* where the user has typed *Castro*, the data will be sent to the server as *Lastname=Castro*.

To divide the data stream into something you can use, you need a CGI script, which is a small computer program, either written by you or copied from another source, that can be activated by clicking a URL.

Unless you know how to program in C or Perl, you may have a hard time using CGI scripts. At the end of this chapter, you'll learn how to start working with CGI, and where you can turn for more information.

Forms

Form structure

Writing the HTML code to make forms is not any more difficult than creating any other element on your web page. Writing the scripts that interpret the data received is a bit more complicated.

To create a form:

1. Type **<FORM**.

2. Type **METHOD="POST"**. You can also use the GET method.

3. Type **ACTION="script.url"** where *script.url* is the location on the server of the CGI script that will be run when the form is submitted.

4. Create the form elements, as described on the following pages.

5. Create a Submit button, as described on page 109. (You don't need to create a submit button if you're using an active image.)

6. Type **</FORM>** to complete the form.

✔ Tip

■ You can use tables to set up your form elements. (See pages 85-99 for more information on tables.)

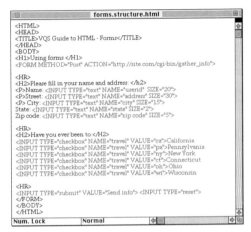

Figure 7-1. *Every form has three parts: the FORM tag, the actual form elements, where the user enters information, and the SUBMIT tag which creates the button that sends the collected information to the server (or an active image).*

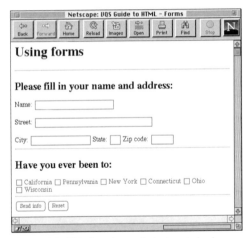

Figure 7-2. *This form has only text and check boxes. It could also contain radio buttons, menus, larger text entry areas, and an active image.*

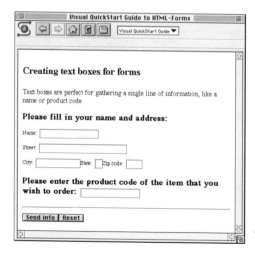

```
forms.textboxes.html
<HTML>
<HEAD>
<TITLE>Visual QuickStart Guide to HTML-Forms</TITLE>
</HEAD>
<BODY>
<H1>Creating text boxes for forms </H1>
<P>Text boxes are perfect for gathering a single line of information, like a
name or product code.
<FORM METHOD="Post" ACTION="http://site.com/cgi-
bin/gather_textboxes">
<H2>Please fill in your name and address: </h2>
<P>Name: <INPUT TYPE="text" NAME="userid" SIZE="20">
<P>Street: <INPUT TYPE="text" NAME="address" SIZE="30">
<P> City: <INPUT TYPE="text" NAME="city" SIZE="15">
State: <INPUT TYPE="text" NAME="state" SIZE="2">
Zip code: <INPUT TYPE="text" NAME="zip code" SIZE="5">
<H2>Please enter the product code of the item that you wish to order:
<INPUT TYPE="text" NAME="productID">
<P>
<HR>
<INPUT TYPE="submit" VALUE="Send info"> <INPUT TYPE="reset">
</FORM>
</BODY>
</HTML>
Num. Lock          Normal
```

Figure 7-3. *Each text box is defined with its own INPUT line.*

Figure 7-4. *Place text boxes on separate lines by adding a <P> between them.*

Figure 7-5. *The spacing in Mosaic's forms (left) is slightly different from that of Netscape's (above left).*

Text boxes

Text boxes contain one line of text and are typically used for names, addresses and the like.

To create a text box:

1. Inside the FORM area of your HTML document, type the title of the text box (for example, **Name:**), if desired.

2. Type **<INPUT TYPE="text"**.

3. Give the text box a name by adding **NAME="name"**. When the data is collected by the server, the information entered in this text box will be identified by the *name*.

4. If desired, define the size of the box on your form, by typing **SIZE="n"**, replacing *n* with the desired width of the box, measured in characters. The default value is 20. Users can add more text than fits in the text box, up to the value defined for **MAXLENGTH**. (See next step.)

5. If desired, define the maximum number of characters that can be entered in the box by typing **MAXLENGTH="n"**, replacing *n* with the desired maximum length in characters.

6. Finish the text box by typing a final **>**.

Password boxes

A password box is similar to a text box, but when the user types in it, the letters are hidden by bullets or asterisks.

To create password entry boxes:

1. Inside the FORM area of your HTML document, type the title of the password box, if desired. Something like **Enter password** will do fine.

2. Type **<INPUT TYPE="password"**.

3. Give the password box a name by typing **NAME="name"**. When the data is collected by the server, the information entered in this password box will be identified by the *name*.

4. If desired, define the size of the box on your form, by typing **SIZE="n"**, replacing *n* with the desired width of the box, measured in characters.

5. If desired, define the maximum number of characters that can be entered in the box by typing **MAXLENGTH="n"**, replacing *n* with the desired value.

6. Finish the text box by typing a final **>**.

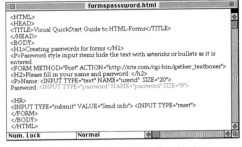

Figure 7-6. *The* VALUE *tag identifies the data once it is posted to the URL. It may or may not be the same as the identifying text that the user sees on screen.*

Figure 7-7. *When the user enters a password in a form viewed with Netscape, the password is hidden with bullets.*

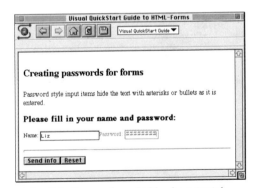

Figure 7-8. *Passwords are hidden by a special character in Mosaic.*

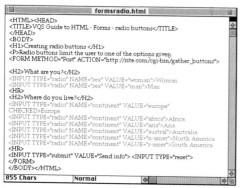

```
formsradio.html
<HTML><HEAD>
<TITLE>VQS Guide to HTML - Forms - radio buttons</TITLE>
</HEAD>
<BODY>
<H1>Creating radio buttons </H1>
<P>Radio buttons limit the user to one of the options given.
<FORM METHOD="Post" ACTION="http://site.com/cgi-bin/gather_buttons">

<H2>What are you?</H2>
<INPUT TYPE="radio" NAME="sex" VALUE="woman">Woman
<INPUT TYPE="radio" NAME="sex" VALUE="man">Man
<HR>
<H2>Where do you live?</H2>
<INPUT TYPE="radio" NAME="continent" VALUE="europe"
CHECKED>Europe
<INPUT TYPE="radio" NAME="continent" VALUE="africa">Africa
<INPUT TYPE="radio" NAME="continent" VALUE="asia">Asia
<INPUT TYPE="radio" NAME="continent" VALUE="austral">Australia
<INPUT TYPE="radio" NAME="continent" VALUE="n-amer">North America
<INPUT TYPE="radio" NAME="continent" VALUE="s-amer">South America
<HR>
<INPUT TYPE="submit" VALUE="Send info"> <INPUT TYPE="reset">
</FORM>
</BODY></HTML>

855 Chars          Normal
```

Figure 7-9. *Radio buttons are linked by a common value for the NAME tag: both elements in the first group have a NAME of* sex *while the elements in the second group have a NAME of* continent.

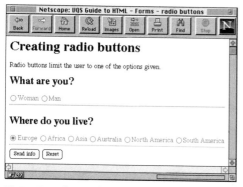

Figure 7-10 (Netscape). *In the first set of radio buttons, there is no "most common" answer; thus, no default has been set with the CHECKED tag.*

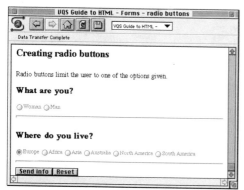

Figure 7-11 (Mosaic). *If most users of this page are from Europe, it is a good idea to use the CHECKED tag to select it by default.*

Radio buttons

Remember those old-time car radios with big black plastic buttons? Push one to listen to WAQY; push another for WRNX. You can never push two buttons at once. Radio buttons on forms work the same way (except you can't listen to the radio). Out of all the radio buttons with the same name, only one can be active at a time. In addition, each radio button must have a value.

To create a radio button:

1. In the FORM area of your HTML document, type the introductory text for your radio buttons. You might choose something like **Select one of the following**.

2. Type **<INPUT TYPE="radio"**.

3. Type **NAME="radioset"** where *radioset* identifies each radio button in a particular set. Only one radio button in a set can be checked.

4. You must define a value for each radio button. Type **VALUE="value"**, where *value* is the data that will be sent to the server if the radio button is checked.

5. If desired, type **CHECKED** to make the radio button active by default when the page is opened.

6. Type the final **>** to finish the radio button definition.

7. Type the text that identifies the radio button to the user. This is often the same as **VALUE**, but needn't be.

8. Repeat steps 2-7 for each radio button in the set.

Check boxes

While radio buttons can accept only one answer per set, a user can check as many check boxes in a set as they like. Like radio buttons, check boxes are linked by their name.

To create check boxes:

1. In the FORM area of your HTML document, type the introductory text for your check boxes. You might choose something like **Select one or more of the following**.

2. Type **<INPUT TYPE="checkbox"** (Notice there is no space in the attribute *checkbox*.)

3. It is a good idea to define a value for each check box. The value will only be sent to the server if the check box is checked (either by the user or by you, see step 4). Type **VALUE= "default value"**. This is often the same as the value shown to the user, but it can be different. (See step 6.)

4. Type **CHECKED** to make the check box checked by default when the page is opened. You (or the user) may check as many check boxes as you wish.

5. Type the final **>** to finish the check box definition.

6. Type the text that identifies the check box to the user. This is often the same as the **VALUE**, but it doesn't have to be.

7. Repeat steps 2-6 for each check box in the set.

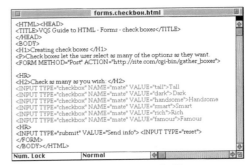

Figure 7-12. *Check boxes are linked by a common NAME. The user may check as many as they wish.*

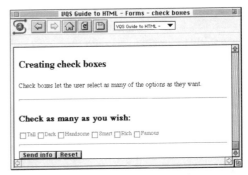

Figure 7-13 (Netscape). *Users can check as many of the options in a set of check boxes as they wish.*

Figure 7-14. *Mosaic really jams form elements up against each other.*

Check boxes

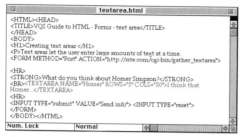

Figure 7-15. *Use a default text that helps your user to fill out the rest of the text box.*

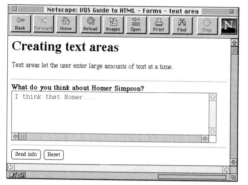

Figure 7-16. *Use a column width of about 50 (COLS="50") if you want the text area to span a normal sized Web page as viewed with Netscape.*

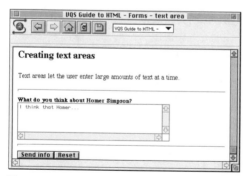

Figure 7-17. *A column width of 50 doesn't quite span a page in Mosaic; a value of 65 almost reaches the right margin.*

Text blocks

In some cases, you want to give the user a larger space to respond. Text blocks may be as large as your page, and will expand as needed if the user enters more text than can fit in the display area.

To create text blocks:

1. In the FORM area of your HTML document, type the introductory text for your text area, if desired.

2. Type **<TEXTAREA**.

3. Type **NAME="name"** where *name* is the variable name you give to your text area. The name identifies the data when it is collected by the server.

4. If desired, type **ROWS="n"**, where *n* is the height of the text area in rows. The default value is 4.

5. If desired, type **COLS="n"**, where *n* is the width of the text area in characters. The default value is 40.

6. Type **>**.

7. Type the default text, if any, for the text area. You may not add any HTML coding here.

8. Type **</TEXTAREA>** to complete the text area.

✔ Tips

■ Users can enter up to 32,700 characters in a text area. Scroll bars will appear when necessary.

Menus

Creating menus for your users makes it easy for them to enter information or provide criteria for a search.

To create menus:

1. In the FORM area of your HTML document, type the introductory text for your menu, if desired.

2. Type **<SELECT**.

3. Type **NAME="name"** where *name* is the variable name for the menu that will identify the data when it is collected by the server.

4. Type **SIZE="n"** where *n* represents the number of items that should be initially visible in the menu.

5. If desired, type **MULTIPLE** to allow the user to select more than one option from the menu.

6. Type the final **>** to finish the menu definition.

7. Type **<OPTION**.

8. Type **SELECTED** if you want the option to be selected by default.

9. Type **VALUE="value"** where *value* is the name that will identify the data when it is collected by the server.

10. Type **>**.

11. Type the option name as you wish it to appear in the menu.

12. Repeat steps 7-11 for each option.

13. Type **</SELECT>**.

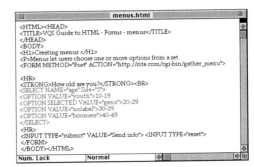

Figure 7-18. *Notice that the option values need not match what the user sees (e.g., youth vs. 10-19). You can use whatever variable name that makes analyzing the information easier.*

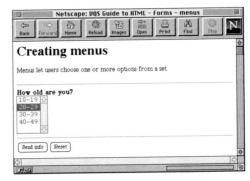

Figure 7-19 (Netscape). *The option with the SELECTED tag is automatically checked when the user jumps to this page.*

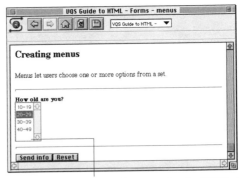

Figure 7-20. *When you choose a value for SIZE that is greater than the number of options available, an empty option appears which allows the user to deselect whatever option(s) were previously selected.*

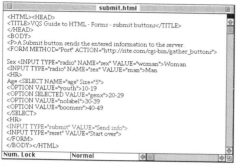

Figure 7-21. *You can use any text you wish for the Submit button. Just make it clear that a click will send the information gathered to the server.*

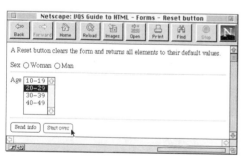

Figure 7-22. *Once the user has entered the appropriate information, they click on the submit button to send the information to the server.*

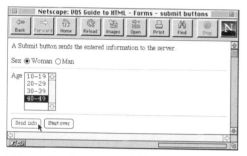

Figure 7-23. *A click on the reset button clears the form and returns all variables to their default values. In this case, there is no default for Sex and so it returns to its unchecked state. The default for Age was 20-29.*

Gathering the information

All the information that your users enter won't be any good to you unless they send it to the server. You should always create a SUBMIT button for your forms so that the user can deliver the information to you. (If you use active images, see page 111.)

To create a submit button:

1. Type **<INPUT TYPE="submit"**.

2. If desired, type **VALUE="submit message"** where *submit message* is the text that will appear in the button. The default submit message is *Submit Query*.

3. Type the final **>**.

Resetting the form

If humans could fill out forms perfectly on the first try, there would be no erasers on pencils and no backspace key on your computer keyboard. You can give your users a Reset button so that they can start over with a fresh form (including all the default values you've set).

To create a Reset button:

1. Type **<INPUT TYPE="reset"**.

2. If desired, type **VALUE="reset message"** where *reset message* is the text that appears in the button. The default reset message is *Reset*.

3. Type **>**.

Submit and Reset buttons

Hidden elements

At first glance, creating hidden elements in a form seems counter productive. How can the user enter information if they can't see where to put it? Actually, they can't. However, hidden elements can be used by you to store information gathered from an *earlier* form so that it can be combined with the present form's data.

For example, if you ask for a user's name in an earlier form, you can save it in a variable and then add it to a new form as a hidden element so that the name is related to the new information gathered without having to bother the user to enter the name several times.

To create a hidden element:

1. Type **<INPUT TYPE="hidden"**.

2. Type **NAME="name"** where *name* is the name of the information to be stored.

3. Type **VALUE="value"** where *value* is the information itself that is to be stored.

4. Type **>**.

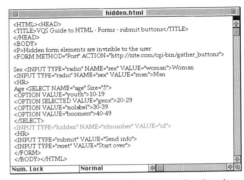

Figure 7-24. *The Hidden element can be placed anywhere in the BODY section of the HTML document.*

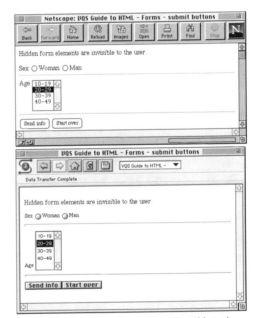

Figure 7-25. *Hidden elements are invisible to the user in all browsers, including Netscape (middle screen) and Mosaic (above).*

Figure 7-26. *You don't need to include a submit button with an active image since a click will automatically submit the data.*

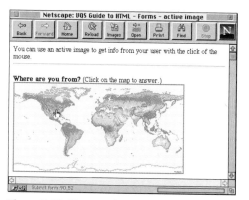

Figure 7-27. *Netscape shows the hand cursor when the user drags it over an active image. In addition, it gives the present coordinates of the mouse in the lower left corner of the window. It is these coordinates that will be sent to the server when the user clicks the mouse button.*

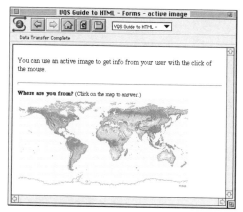

Figure 7-28. *Active images are not as clear in Mosaic; the cursor does not change shape and no coordinates are shown.*

Active images

You may use images as active elements in a FORM area. A click on the image appends the current mouse coordinates (as measured from the top left corner) to the variable name and sends the data to the server.

To create an active image:

1. Create a GIF image and save it in your images directory on your server. (See page 31.)

2. Type **<INPUT TYPE="image"**.

3. Type **SRC="image_url"** where *image_url* is the location of the image on the server.

4. Type **NAME="name"**. When the user clicks on the image, the x and y coordinates of the mouse will be appended to the name defined here and sent to the server.

5. Type the final **>** to finish the active image definition for the FORM.

✔ Tips

■ All the form data is sent automatically when the user clicks on the active image. Therefore, it's a good idea to give instructions on how to use the active image and to place the image at the end of the form so that the user completes the other form elements before clicking the image and sending the data.

■ You can create an entire questionnaire out of pictures by making the next question (and active image) appear after the data is sent from the last question to the server.

Active images

CGI scripts

A Common Gateway Interface (CGI) script, or gateway program, is an actual program (or batch file) that can be activated by the user with a click on a URL. It may be written in a computer language like C or Pascal, or it may be written in Perl or a shell program, and be a simple executable.

The advantage of using Perl or a shell program is that the script can be easily ported from computer to computer and doesn't need to be compiled. In other words, you can copy a Perl script from someone else, adapt it to your needs by changing the appropriate paths and incorporate it into your page.

One of the principal uses of CGI scripts in HTML documents is to analyze, parse and store information received from a form, but their more general use is to interact with the server, storing and requesting data, and then offering the results to the user.

The results that are reported back to the user are often formatted as a new HTML document, using the same tags that you've been learning throughout this book.

You need certain permissions to use CGI scripts on particular servers. Any time you open communication between the server and the public (e.g. your users) you are putting the server at a security risk. You should speak to your system administrator about what you need to do to use CGI.

Figure 7-29. *You can test your scripts with a Telnet program. If they don't work here, they won't work when your user points to them.*

Figure 7-30. *This is a simple script that creates an HTML page, queries the server for the date, and inserts that date in the HTML page.*

Figure 7-31. *To use the script, create a link to it in your HTML page.*

Figure 7-32. *The simple HTML page in Netscape shows the link to the script.*

Figure 7-33. *Since the script includes HTML coding, the result is an HTML page that contains the date.*

Using CGI scripts

A CGI script is used to activate programs on the server to get information and then to report that information to the user. For example, you could use a CGI script to call the date program on the server and report the results on a Web page.

To create a link to a CGI script:

1. In your HTML document, type **<A HREF="http://www.site.com/** where *www.site.com* is the name of the server that contains the CGI script.

2. Type **cgi-bin**, where *cgi-bin* is the location of CGI scripts on most UNIX servers.

3. Type **/path** where *path* is the path to the cgi-script, if it is not found directly in the main cgi-bin directory. For example, on many servers, each user has their own cgi-bin directory within their personal directory.

4. Type **/cgiscript** where *cgiscript* is the name of the cgiscript that you wish to call.

5. Type **>**.

6. Type the clickable text that the user will click to activate the script.

7. Type **</A>** to complete the link.

MULTIMEDIA

One of the things that has made the Web so popular is the idea that you can add graphics, sound and movies to your Web pages. The truth is that today's browsers can only show two kinds of graphic images inline, at most, and that they rely on external applications called *helpers* to open other types of multimedia files. (Of course, the technology is moving so fast that tomorrow's browsers, or perhaps even this afternoon's browsers, may in fact be able to handle more complicated multimedia files without helpers.)

The main problem with multimedia is that the files are generally very large. Ten seconds of average quality sound take up more than 200K, which will take your user three and a half minutes to download before they can hear it with the helper program. Ten seconds of a movie displayed in a tiny 2" x 3" window are considerably larger. Similarly, large still images (even if they are JPEG or GIF format) can exhaust your users.

Finally, since the Web population is diverse, and uses many different kinds of computers, you have to make sure that the files you provide can be read by your users (or the largest number possible of them). This is probably the trickiest part of all.

Multimedia

Helper applications

If a browser cannot handle a certain type of file, it calls up a "helper application" to view the file. A helper application can be any program that is capable of opening the particular format of the file.

For example, a user could conceivably use Adobe Photoshop as a helper application to view TIFF images. But since Photoshop is such a complete program, it takes several seconds to load and view the image—not to mention the fact that it costs $900. Users are generally better off with a small, fast, free, helper application that is good at just one thing: viewing or playing specific file formats. See Table 8-1 for a list of common helper applications.

A browser can only call a helper application if two conditions are met. First, the user must already have the helper application on the computer (*and* have specified which helper application to use for which types of files).

Although helper applications are easily acquired through many FTP servers, not all users have taken the time to download them. If your users don't have the proper helper application, they won't be able to view your files.

Second, you, the page designer, must use the proper extension for the file so that the browser knows which helper application will be necessary to access the file. The system of standardized extensions is known as MIME—Multipurpose Internet Mail Extensions. (See Table 8-1.)

Mime type	Extension
image/gif	.gif
image/jpeg	.jpeg .jpg .jpe
image/pict	.pic .pict
image/tiff	.tif .tiff
image/x-xbitmap	.xbm
audio/basic	.au .snd
audio/aiff	.aiff .aif
audio/x-wav	.wav
video/quicktime	.qt .mov
video/mpeg	.mpg .mpeg .mpe
video/x-msvideo	.avi
application/mac-binhex40	.hqx
application/x-stuffit	.sit
application/x-macbinary	.bin
application/octet-stream	.exe
application/postscript	.ai .eps .ps
application/rtf	.rtf
application/x-compressed	.zip .z .gz .tgz
application/x-tar	.tar

Table 8-1. *It is extremely important to use the proper extension to identify your external files. If there is more than one possible extension, you can generally use whichever you prefer, as long as you follow the naming limitations of the server (e.g. DOS servers insist on three letter extensions).*

	Mac	Windows	Unix
Graphics	JPEGView	LView Pro	xv
		PaintShop Pro	
Sound	SoundMachine	Wham	audiotool
	SoundApp	Wplany	audioplayer
Video	Sparkle	Media Player	mpeg_play
	Fast Player	mpegplay	xplaygizmo
Postscript		ghostscript	ghostscript
		ghostview	ghostview

Table 8-2. *Some common helper applications.*

Helper applications

Figure 8-3. *Since a user has to take the time to download large images like the one referenced here, you should at least give them an idea of how big the image is.*

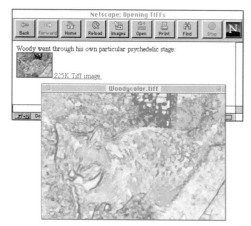

Figure 8-4. *Once the user clicks on the icon, the browser launches the helper application (in this case JPEGView) and the helper application shows the TIFF file.*

Non-GIF/JPEG images

You learned how to create links to external GIF or JPEG graphics in Chapter 3, but what about other formats? As long as you use the proper extension (so the browser knows what kind of graphic it is) and the user has a helper application that can view the image, you can create a link to any kind of graphic file you want.

To create a link to a non-GIF or non-JPEG image:

1. Create an image and save it in the desired format with the proper extension. (See Table 8-1 on page 116.)

2. In your HTML document where you want the image to appear, type **<A HREF="image.ext">** where *image.ext* is the name of the image file on the server with the appropriate extension.

3. If desired, use a icon to indicate the external image by typing **<IMG SRC="icon.gif">** where *icon.gif* is the location on the server of the icon.

4. Give a description of the image, including its size and format, for example, **2 Mb TIFF image of dolphin**.

5. Complete the link by typing **</A>**.

✔ Tips

- Why bother with other formats besides GIF or JPEG? Perhaps you want to provide non-expert users with a certain type of graphic image (TIFF, say) and you don't want them to have to bother with converting it.

- Since non-GIF/JPEG images will not appear inline, there is no point in using additional image formatting, like ALIGN or LOWSRC.

Sound

Presently, there is only one sound format that can be read by Macs, Windows machines, Unix and others: the au format developed by Sun Microsystems. Unfortunately, the au format only allows for 8 bit sampling, which is certainly at the low end of the quality scale.

The standard format for Macintosh sound is AIFF while Windows machines read sound in the WAV format. You can add sound files to your Web pages in any of these formats, but only those users with the corresponding computer system will be able to download and listen to the sounds right away.

One alternative is to use a conversion program to create several different versions of your sound files and then give your users access to all of them. Then they can download and listen to the one that corresponds to their system.

If your computer has a sound card and microphone (like most Macintosh and many PCs), and you have a sound editing program, you can create your own sound files.

To create a sound on the Mac:

1. Open the Sound control panel **(Figure 8-5)**.

2. Click Add **(Figure 8-5)**.

3. Click Record in the dialog box that appears **(Figure 8-6)**.

4. Record your sound.

5. Click Stop and then Save.

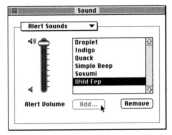

Figure 8-5. *To create a sound with the Macintosh's Sound control panel, click Add.*

Figure 8-6. *Click Record to start recording your sound and Stop when you are finished. Then click Save to save your sound.*

Figure 8-7. *Finally, give your sound a unique name.*

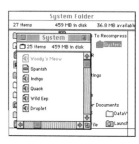

Figure 8-8. *Once you have created the sound, you can find it in the System icon inside the System folder.*

Click here to start recording.

Figure 8-9. *The Sound Recorder main window in Windows.*

Figure 8-10. *Be sure and choose the appropriate format in the pop-up menu when you save your sound.*

6. Give the sound a name and click OK **(Figure 8-7)**.

7. Close the Sound control panel.

8. Open the System Folder and then double click the System icon. You'll find your new sound here **(Figure 8-8)**.

To create a sound in Windows:

1. Open Sound Recorder **(Figure 8-9)**.

2. Click on the microphone icon at the far right **(Figure 8-9)**.

3. Start recording your sound.

4. Click Stop (the button with the square) to finish recording.

5. Choose Save as in the File menu to save your sound file.

6. Choose the appropriate format for the file in the Save as dialog box, and make sure the appropriate extension (.au for au files, .aif for AIFF files, and .wav for WAV files) is added to the file name **(Figure 8-10)**.

✔ Tip

■ Creating sounds for other systems is essentially the same process as outlined here, using the sound editor appropriate to that system.

Creating sound

Converting sounds from one format to another

Once you have a sound, you need to convert it to the proper format for publication on the Web. Although the au format can be understood by many different kinds of computers, the quality is not that great. Therefore, you may want to provide several versions of your sound file: one in au, one in AIFF for Macintosh, and one in WAV for Windows.

To convert a sound from one format to another:

1. Open SoundApp (for Macintosh) or some other sound conversion program (like Wham for Windows).

2. Choose Convert in the File menu **(Figure 8-11)**.

3. Choose the desired sound document in the dialog box that appears. Select a format in the Convert To pop-up menu **(Figure 8-12)**.

4. Click Open.

5. SoundApp places the converted file in a new folder inside the current folder **(Figure 8-14)**.

6. Add the correct extension to the end of the name (even for Macintosh files). Use .au for au files, .aif for AIFF files and .wav for WAV files.

✔ Tip

■ You can convert files from the Finder with SoundApp. Select the files, hold down the Shift key and drag them onto the SoundApp application. You can change the default destination format (and keyboard shortcut) in the Preferences dialog box.

Figure 8-11. *In SoundApp (for Macintosh), choose Convert in the File menu.*

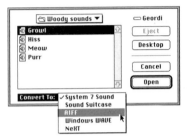

Figure 8-12. *Choose the appropriate format in the Convert To menu.*

Figure 8-13. *SoundApp shows you the progress of the file conversion.*

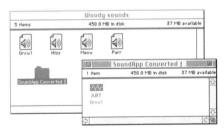

Figure 8-14. *When SoundApp has finished converting the files, it places them in a folder called SoundApp Converted f inside the current folder.*

Converting sounds

Figure 8-15. *Always include information on your page about the size and recording quality of your sound.*

Figure 8-16. *When the user clicks the sound icon (the victrola) or the clickable text description of the sound, the browser downloads the sound and launches the helper application (in this case SoundMachine) which plays the sound.*

Adding sound to a Web page

There is no special trick to adding sound to a Web page. Since no Web browser can currently play sound files without a helper program, you simply add a link to the sound as you would to any other external element. When a user clicks the link, the browser downloads the sound and opens the helper program, which in turn opens and plays the sound file.

It is important to give extra information to your user, including the format and size of the audio file, so that they can decide whether or not to download it.

To add a sound to your page:

1. Create a small icon that you can use as an inline image on your page to indicate the link to the sound and call it *sound.gif.*

2. Make sure the sound file has the correct extension. Otherwise, the user's browser will not know what kind of file it is and may be unable to find a suitable helper. (Use .au for au files, .aif for AIFF files and .wav for WAV files.)

3. In your HTML document where you wish to place the link to the sound file, type **<A HREF="sound.ext">** where *sound.ext* is the location of the sound file, including the correct extension, on the server.

4. Type **<IMG SRC="soundicon.gif">** where *soundicon.gif* is the icon that will indicate the link to the sound.

5. Type the description, size and format of the audio file.

6. Type **</A>** to complete the link to the sound.

Video

If you listen to the Web hype long enough, you'll believe you can tune into Paramount's home page and watch previews to their new movies. Unfortunately, thanks to the huge size of video files and the relative minuscule speed of most home modems, although you might be *able* to do this, you might be gray before the opening credits finish rolling.

Nevertheless, it is possible to add links to video on your Web pages. As with sound files, you have to be especially careful to provide video in a format that your users will be able to use: QuickTime and MPEG for Mac and Windows, AVI just for Windows.

Capturing video

If you have an AV Mac or PowerMac or a video capture card for your PC, you can create video files by copying clips from your VCR to your computer. Along with the video-specific hardware, you will need a fast computer and a big, fast, hard disk.

The actual process, although not difficult, is a bit beyond the scope of this book. Your AV Mac or Video card should have instructions on how to digitize video. In my experience, the hardest part is figuring out where to connect all the cables.

Once again, you have to be careful about just what you copy. Most broadcast television is copyrighted and may not be published without permission. Of course, you are welcome to insert videos on your page that you've filmed yourself.

You may also find video files online or in a commercial library on CD-ROM.

Figure 8-17. *You can use Adobe Premiere with an AV Mac or a PC with video capture card to capture video from a VCR.*

Figure 8-18. *If you don't have your own home movies, you can use copyright free clips included in CD-ROM collections, like this short movie, which is included in the Adobe Premiere Deluxe CD-ROM.*

Figure 8-19. *These tiny menus reveal the simplicity of many video conversion programs. FastPlayer (left) flattens Macintosh QuickTime movies for viewing on Windows machines. AVI->QT (right) converts AVI format movies to QuickTime format.*

Converting video to the proper format

Your users will only be able to download and view your video files if you have saved them in the proper format, with the proper extension.

To convert video to the proper format:

1. Open a video conversion program.

2. Open the video file.

3. Choose Save as in the File menu **(Figure 8-19)**.

4. In the Format submenu, choose QuickTime, AVI or MPEG. QuickTime and MPEG movies can be viewed on both Macintosh and Windows machines. AVI movies are only for Windows.

5. Give the new movie file a distinct name and the proper extension (.qt or .mov for QuickTime, .avi for AVI and .mpeg or .mpg for MPEG).

6. Click Save.

✔ Tip

■ In addition, QuickTime movies need to be *flattened* before they can be viewed on other types of computers besides Macintosh. Use a tool like FastPlayer (for Mac) or Qflat (for Windows).

Adding video to your page

There is no browser that can currently view video without a helper application. Therefore, to add video to your Web page you must make a link to your video file. When the user clicks the link, the browser downloads the video file and opens the appropriate helper program which then views the video.

To add a link to video:

1. Create a small icon that you can use as an inline image on your page to indicate the link to the video and call it *video.gif*.

2. Make sure the video file has the correct extension (even for Macintosh files). Otherwise, the user's browser will not know what kind of file it is and may be unable to open it. (Use .qt or .mov for QuickTime files, .avi for AVI files and .mpeg or .mpg for MPEG files.)

3. In your HTML document, where you wish to place the link to the video file, type **<A HREF="video.ext">** where *video.ext* is the location of the video file, including the correct extension, on the server.

4. Type **<IMG SRC="video.gif">** where *video.gif* is the location of the icon that will indicate the link to the video.

5. Type the size and format of the video file, for example, **5.2 Mb QuickTime movie**.

6. Type **</A>** to complete the link to the video file.

Figure 8-20. *It's a good idea to tell your users how big the video file is so that they know how long it will take to download.*

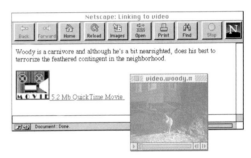

Figure 8-21. *A click by the user on the icon or text launches the video player and plays the video.*

Adding video to your page

EXTRAS 9

In this chapter, you'll find a collection of special touches you can give your Web pages to set them apart from the crowd (or to make them fit in better by following the latest trends).

BEWARE! Some of the HTML tricks offered here, most notably the animated title and the special alternative text, are nonstandard and not supported by all browsers. This kind of code sort of sneaks by the browser trying not to call too much attention to itself. And although it probably can't do much damage, future browsers may be pickier about what you throw at them.

At any rate, you should definitely check out the shortcut for creating HTML tables in Word. Like most shortcuts, it's very simple and yet can save you an enormous amount of time.

The inspiration of others

One of the easiest ways to expand your HTML fluency is by looking at how other page designers have created *their* pages. Luckily, HTML code is easy to view and is not copyrighted. However, text content, graphics, sounds, video and other external files may be copyrighted. As a general rule, use other designers' pages for inspiration with your HTML, and then create your own contents.

To view other designers' HTML code:

1. Open their page with any browser.

2. Choose View Source (in the View menu in Netscape, in the File menu in Mosaic).

3. The browser will open the helper application you have specified for text files and show you the HTML code for the given page.

4. If you wish, save the file with the text editor for further study.

✔ Tip

■ You can also save the source code by selecting Save as in the File menu and then Source or HTML in the Format pop-up menu in the dialog box that appears.

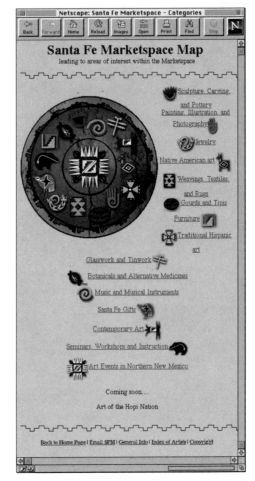

Figure 9-1. *This is one of my favorite pages on the Web. It can be found at http://www.artsantafe.com/sfm/sfmmap.html.*

Figure 9-2. *When you select View Source, the assigned text editor opens with the page's HTML code.*

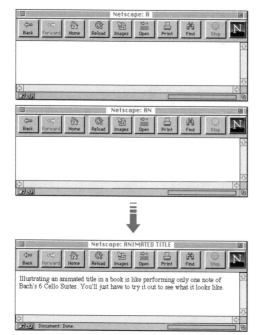

```
animatedtitle.html
<HTML>
<HEAD>
<TITLE>ANIMATED TITLE</TITLE>
<TITLE>ANIMATED TITL</TITLE>
<TITLE>ANIMATED TIT</TITLE>
<TITLE>ANIMATED TI</TITLE>
<TITLE>ANIMATED T</TITLE>
<TITLE>ANIMATED </TITLE>
<TITLE>ANIMATED</TITLE>
<TITLE>ANIMAT</TITLE>
<TITLE>ANIMA</TITLE>
<TITLE>ANIM</TITLE>
<TITLE>ANI</TITLE>
<TITLE>AN</TITLE>
<TITLE>A</TITLE>
<TITLE>AN</TITLE>
<TITLE>ANI</TITLE>
<TITLE>ANIM</TITLE>
<TITLE>ANIMA</TITLE>
<TITLE>ANIMAT</TITLE>
<TITLE>ANIMATE</TITLE>
<TITLE>ANIMATED</TITLE>
<TITLE>ANIMATED </TITLE>
<TITLE>ANIMATED T</TITLE>
<TITLE>ANIMATED TI</TITLE>
<TITLE>ANIMATED TIT</TITLE>
<TITLE>ANIMATED TITL</TITLE>
<TITLE>ANIMATED TITLE</TITLE>
</HEAD>
<BODY>
Illustrating an animated title in a book is like performing only one note of
Bach's 6 Cello Suites. You'll have to try it out to see what it looks like.
```
Num. Lock   Normal

Figure 9-3. *Netscape will read each and every TITLE tag, changing each one as it goes. This makes it appear like the title is growing and receding.*

Netscape: A

Netscape: AN

Netscape: ANIMATED TITLE

Illustrating an animated title in a book is like performing only one note of Bach's 6 Cello Suites. You'll just have to try it out to see what it looks like.

Document : Done.

Figure 9-4. *Illustrating an animated title in a book is like performing only one note (OK, three) of Bach's Cello Suites. You'll just have to try it out to see what it looks like.*

Creating an animated title

NETSCAPE ONLY An animated title may either appear in the title bar one letter at a time or it may appear and disappear continuously. The trick to creating an animated title is using multiple TITLE tags.

To create an animated title that appears one letter at a time:

1. Type **<HTML><HEAD>**.

2. Type **<TITLE>**.

3. Type the first letter of the title.

4. Type **</TITLE>**.

5. Type **<TITLE>**.

6. Type the first and second letters of the title. (If you only type the second letter, you won't see the title *growing*, but rather you'll see each letter appear individually, one after the next.)

7. Type **</TITLE>**.

8. Type **<TITLE>**.

9. Type the first, second and third letters of the title.

10. Type **</TITLE>**.

11. Keep creating new TITLE tags, each with one more letter than the last, until you have completed your title.

12. Type **</HEAD>** and continue with the BODY of your page.

✔ Tip

■ Make the last title the complete version. It will be displayed as the user views the page.

Creating drop caps

Some of the best tricks are the simplest. Since HTML doesn't let you choose a font to set off a drop cap, you can create an image file of the capital letter, make it transparent, and insert it before the rest of the paragraph.

To create a drop cap:

1. In an image editing program, create the capital letter, in any font you choose, for your drop cap. Save it in GIF format and make it transparent. (See pages 31 and 47.)

2. In your HTML document where you want the drop cap to appear, type **<IMG SRC="dropcap.gif"** where *dropcap.gif* is the location on the server of the image created in step 1.

3. Type **ALIGN=left** so that the text that follows wraps around the drop cap.

4. Type the final **>** to finish the IMG definition.

5. Type the text that should appear next to the drop cap. Generally, next to a drop cap, it is is a good idea to type the first few words in all caps.

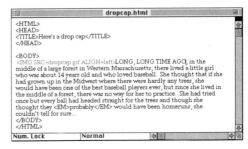

Figure 9-5. *Use the ALIGN=LEFT tag to wrap the text around the drop cap.*

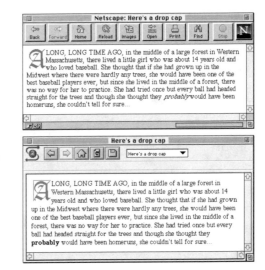

Figure 9-6. *Drop caps (in Netscape, above, and Mosaic) are ideal for books or stories.*

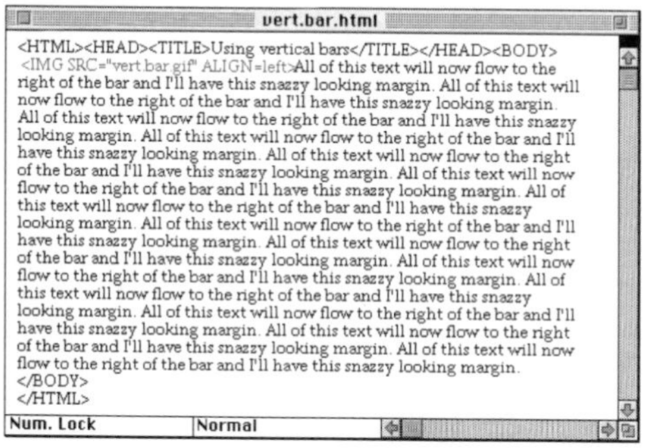

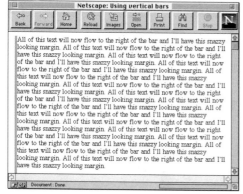

Figure 9-7. *You can create a vertical bar on the left side of the page by inserting an image and using the ALIGN=left attribute.*

Figure 9-8. *It doesn't really matter if the vertical bar is longer than the text. It will simply continue down the page.*

Using vertical rules

It's easy to create horizontal rules in an HTML document. Creating vertical rules, along the left or right margin, for example, is only slightly more complicated.

To create a vertical rule:

1. In Photoshop, or other image editing program, create a bar, of the desired color, 5 pixels wide and 500 pixels high.

2. In the HTML document, place the cursor above the text that should be alongside the vertical bar.

3. Type **<IMG SRC="verticalbar.gif"** where *verticalbar.gif* is the location on the server of the vertical bar created in step 1.

4. *Either* type **ALIGN=left** to place the vertical bar along the left margin *or* type **ALIGN=right** to place it along the right margin.

5. Type the final **>** to complete the IMG definition.

6. Type the text that should appear alongside the vertical rule.

✔ Tip

■ You can widen the margin of your text by inserting a transparent vertical rule on either side of the body of your page. You can also use transparent GIFs to adjust the spacing between paragraphs, and even between words.

Using vertical rules

Special alternative text

You should always use alternative text with your image definitions, just in case your users can't, or have chosen not to view images in their browsers. You don't have to be restricted to a simple description of what the image was, however. You can use images completely made up of ASCII characters.

To create ASCII images of text:

1. Open a browser like Netscape or Mosaic and jump to *http://www.inf. utfsm.cl/cgi-bin/figlet/service.*

2. Enter the word that you wish to convert into an ASCII image.

3. Choose a font from the pop-up menu.

4. Click Process **(Figure 9-9)**.

The figlet server sends back the ASCII image on a fresh page **(Figure 9-10)**.

5. Choose Save as in the File menu **(Figure 9-11)**.

6. Choose Text in the Format menu.

7. Give your ASCII image a name and save it **(Figure 9-12)**.

✔ Tip

■ You can find a slew of ASCII images at *http://search.yahoo.com/bin/ search?p=ascii+art.*

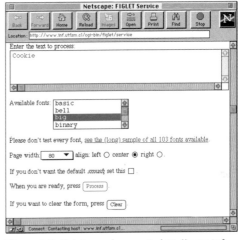

Figure 9-9. *Point your browser to http://www.inf. utfsm.cl/cgi-bin/figlet/service and follow the instructions on the page.*

Figure 9-10. *Once you click the Process button, the figlet server converts your text into an ASCII image.*

Figure 9-11. *Choose Save as in the File menu (in either Netscape or Mosaic) to save the ASCII image.*

Figure 9-12. *Choose Text for the format, give your ASCII image a name and save it.*

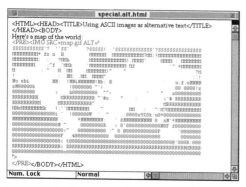

Figure 9-13. *Keep in mind that ASCII images rely on monospaced fonts. (To make the illustration appear correctly in this book, I had to format the characters in my text editor with a monospaced font.)*

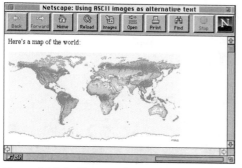

Figure 9-14. *In Netscape, the regular image shows as usual.*

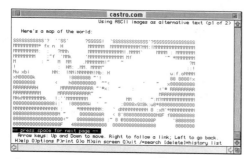

Figure 9-15. *In Lynx, which cannot show the regular image, you see the alternative text.*

Using special alternative text

Once you've found some alternative text that says what you want with a flair, there are some tricks to keeping it in shape in your HTML document.

To use special alternative text:

1. Type **<PRE>**. Inserting the PRE tag before the IMG tag assures that the special alternative text will be formatted properly. You may not include the PRE tag inside the IMG tag.

2. Type **<IMG SRC="image.gif"** where *image.gif* is the location of the image on the server.

3. If desired, add other image attributes.

4. Type **ALT="**. Press Return.

5. Type, or better yet copy and paste, the special alternative text.

6. Press Return.

7. Type **">** to complete the alternative text and IMG tag.

8. Type **</PRE>**.

✔ Tips

- If you copy the text from some other source, be sure it doesn't contain any double quotes since they will complete the ALT attribute prematurely.

- This trick works best with Lynx. The alternative text doesn't load quite right in Netscape or Mosaic.

Using special alternative text

A shortcut for creating HTML tables in Word

Creating tables by hand can be a pain. It's hard to see where to put each element and you have to type TD and TR over and over again. Here's a clever way to convert a table from Word (both Mac and Windows versions) into an HTML table.

To convert a Word table into HTML:

1. Create a table in a separate document using Microsoft Word (for Macintosh or Windows).

2. Select the entire table and choose Table to text in the Format menu.

3. In the dialog box that appears, choose Tab delimited.

Your table now consists of individual paragraphs (which correspond to each row) separated by returns. Each element is separated by a tab.

4. With the cursor at the top of the document, select Find/Change in the Edit menu (Command-H).

5. In the Find box, type **^p** to search for every occurrence of a new paragraph (that is a new row).

6. In the Change box, type **</TD> </TR>^p<TR>** (without spaces). The ^p is optional, since extra returns will be ignored by the browser. It simply makes the HTML document easier to read (and edit).

7. Click Change all.

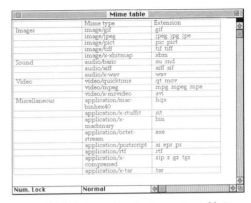

Figure 9-16. *It is much easier to create a table in Microsoft Word than with Table tags.*

Figure 9-17. *Select Table to text in the Insert menu.*

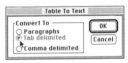

Figure 9-18. *Choose Tab delimited in the Table to text dialog box.*

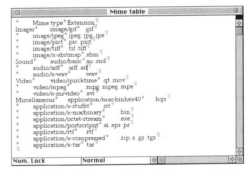

Figure 9-19. *Each row of the table is converted into a separate paragraph. The elements in each row are separated by tabs.*

Creating HTML tables in Word

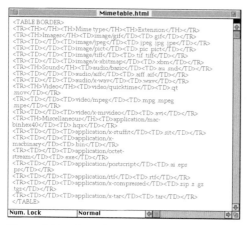

Figure 9-20. *After a few search and replace operations, the table is transformed into HTML code.*

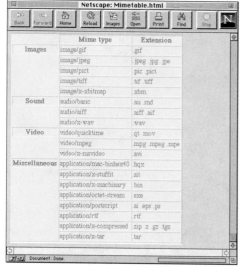

Figure 9-21. *The table looks great in Netscape.*

8. In the Find box, type **^t** to search for every occurrence of a tab (a new element).

9. In the Change box, type **</TD><TD>**.

10. Click Change all.

11. At the very beginning of the document, type **<TABLE>**. Include any table attributes, as desired. (See pages 89-98.)

12. Type **<TR><TD>**.

13. At the very end of the document, you may find extra blank lines of TRs and TDs. Eliminate them. Then type **</TABLE>** after the final </TD></TR>.

14. Change the TDs of your header cells to THs as needed (yes, sorry, by hand).

15. Choose Save as in the File menu and Text Only in the Format submenu of the dialog box that appears. Click OK.

16. Copy the table back into your HTML document.

17. View your table to make sure that everything is the way you want it. You may want to adjust the alignment or text formatting of individual cells.

✔ **Tip**

■ Save frequently and sequentially! If you decide to add a column to your table, it will help to have a copy of the Word table still lying around.

Creating HTML tables in Word

PUBLISHING

Once you've finished your master-piece and are ready to present it to the public, you have to publish your page on a server and help your public find a way to your door.

Your first step is to organize your files, designate a home page and then test everything and make sure it works like you planned.

Then you're ready to transfer the files to the server and to change the permissions so that the files are open to the public.

Finally, you should use the services available on the Web to advertise your page so that your readers know where to find you.

Publishing

Organizing files for transfer

Before transferring your files to the server, you should organize them in one or more folders or directories.

To organize your files for transfer:

1. Create a central folder or directory to hold all the material that will be available at your Web site. (On the Mac, choose New Folder in the File menu in the Finder. On Windows, choose Create Directory in the File menu of the File Manager. In DOS, type **mkdir**.)

2. Give the folder or directory a short, descriptive name.

3. Drag all the HTML files, images and external files that belong to your Web site to the new folder/directory. (In DOS, use the **move** command.)

4. Organize the central folder/directory. You may decide to create a separate folder for HTML documents, one for images and one for other external files. If you have a large site with many pages, you may wish to divide the site into categories or chapters as I've done here, placing the images in the individual folders.

The names and paths should correspond to the links you have established in your pages.

✔ Tip

■ Use simple, one-word names without symbols or punctuation for your files and folders. Use a consistent scheme of capital and small letters. This helps make your URLs easier to type and your pages easier to reach.

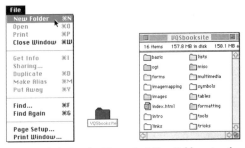

Figure 10-1. *On the Mac, select New Folder, give the folder a name, and then drag each HTML document to the new folder.*

Figure 10-2. *In Windows, select Create Directory in the File menu...*

...give the new directory a name...

...and then drag the HTML documents to the new directory.

Organizing files for transfer

Figure 10-3. *On a Macintosh, change the name of the home page to* index.html *and place it in the main folder of the Web site.*

Figure 10-4. *In Windows, change the name of the home page to* index.htm *and place it in the main directory of the Web site.*

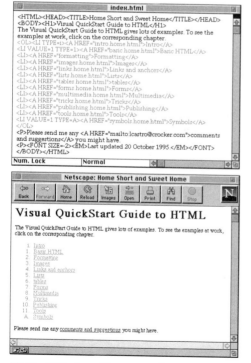

Figure 10-5. *A good home page draws the users right into the material, giving them easy, quick access.*

Designating a home page

A home page is the one that a user will see if they use a URL without a file name. That is, if your site's principal directory on the server is *www.site.com/flintstone/website1*, and a user points to *http://www.site.com/flintstone/website1/*, with a trailing forward slash but no file name, the browser will look for the default or home page. The most common home page name is *index.html* but varies from server to server. Ask your server administrator to be sure.

To designate one page as the home page:

1. Change the file name of the page to *index.html* (or whatever the default home page name is for your server).

2. Place the home page in the principal directory of your web site.

✔ Tips

■ Your home page should have links to all the other information available at your Web site. Your home page should be a table of contents to your site, not just the first page.

■ If you want your users to be able to reach the other pages in your site, make your home page clean, neat and fast **(Figure 10-5)**.

■ If you work on a Windows or DOS machine and with a UNIX server, you will have to transfer the file to the server first, and then add the four letter extension.

Testing your page

Even if you use a validation command in a special HTML editor (see page 150) to check your HTML documents for proper syntax, you should always test your HTML pages in at least one browser. It is not necessary to connect to the server to test your pages. Instead, use the Open Local or Open File command to open the pages from your local computer.

Inevitably you will have to make adjustments to your HTML code. You only need to forget one angle bracket for your page to look completely different from what you expected. Other times what you thought might look OK looks awful.

To test your HTML pages:

1. Before you copy your file to the server, view it locally on your own computer by choosing Open Local or Open File **(Figure 10-6)** in the browser's File menu. (Viewing files locally saves connection charges.)

2. Go through the whole page and make sure it looks exactly the way you want it. For example:

a. Is the formatting like you wanted?

b. Does each of your URLs point to the proper document? (You can check the URLs by clicking them if the destination files are located in the same relative position on the local computer.)

c. Are your images aligned properly?

d. Have you included your name and e-mail address (preferably in a mailto URL) so that your users can contact you with comments and suggestions?

Figure 10-6. *Use the Open File or Open Local file command (depending on your program) to open the file in your local computer to test it.*

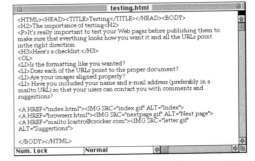

Figure 10-7. *Check your document for typographical errors, missing angle brackets, and other mistakes.*

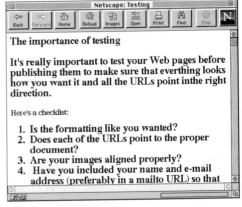

Figure 10-8. *Can you tell what's making this page look so bad?*

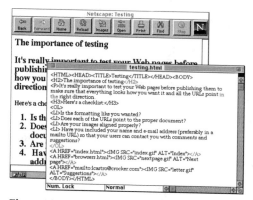

Figure 10-9. *As long as you have enough memory, you can keep the browser and the text editor open at the same time so that you can see what effects your changes are having.*

Figure 10-10. *You must save the changes to your HTML document before reloading, or else the changes will not appear in the browser.*

Figure 10-11. *Select Reload (in the View menu in Netscape; in the Navigate menu in Mosaic), or click the Reload button in the main window to view the changes.*

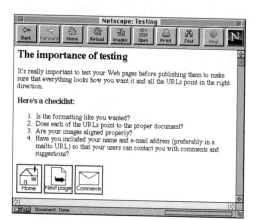

Figure 10-12. *After reloading the fixed HTML document, everything appears as it should—artistic deficiencies aside.*

3. Without closing the page on the browser, open the text or HTML editor and the corresponding HTML document. You should be able to simultaneously edit the HTML document with one program and view it with another **(Figure 10-9)**.

4. Save the changes **(Figure 10-10)**.

5. Switch back to the browser and choose Reload (usually Command-R) to see the changes **(Figures 10-11 and 10-12)**.

6. Repeat steps 1-5 until you are satisfied with your Web page. Don't get discouraged if it takes several tries.

7. Transfer the files to the server and change the permissions, if you haven't done so already. (See pages 140-143.)

8. Test all your URLs to make sure that they work correctly from the server.

✔ **Tip**

■ Use several browsers to test your HTML documents. You never know what browser your user is going to use. The three principal browsers are discussed on pages xv-xvi.

Testing your page

Transferring files to the server

The steps you need to take to transfer files to the server depend on the type of server you are working with and where it is located. If your server is a Macintosh or Windows machine down the hall, you simply copy the files to the appropriate folder or directory on that computer.

Most people, however, use UNIX servers at a remote location. The easiest way to transfer your HTML files to this kind of server is an FTP program, like Fetch for Macintosh (see below), or WS_FTP for Windows (see pages 142-143).

To transfer HTML files to the server with Fetch:

1. Open your Internet connection.

2. Open Fetch or some other FTP program.

3. Choose Preferences in the Customize menu **(Figure 10-13)**, Uploading in the Topics menu of the Preferences box that appears and make sure the Add file format suffixes option is not checked **(Figure 10-14)**.

4. Select Open Connection in the main window to show the Open Connection window **(Figure 10-15)**.

5. Enter the server name in the Host text box, your user name in the User ID box, your password in the Password box and the path to the directory where you plan to save the Web pages in the Directory box **(Figure 10-16)**.

6. Click OK to open the connection.

Fetch will make the connection to the server you requested and open the designated directory.

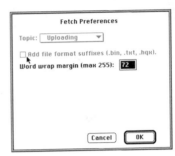

Figure 10-13. *Choose Preferences in Fetch's Customize menu to open the Preferences dialog box.*

Figure 10-14. *Choose Uploading in the Topic menu and then unmark the Add file format suffixes option.*

Figure 10-15. *Click the Open Connection button or select the Open Connection in the File menu to display the Open Connection window.*

Figure 10-16. *In the Open Connection window, type the server name (Host) your User ID and password and the directory where you want to transfer the files.*

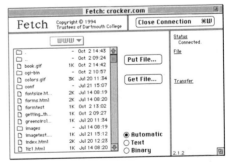

Figure 10-17. *Make sure the proper directory on the server (where you want to transfer the files) is showing in the Fetch window before transferring the files (in this case, WWW).*

Figure 10-18. *Choose Put Folders and Files in the Remote menu. (To transfer just one file, you can click the Put File button in the main Fetch window.)*

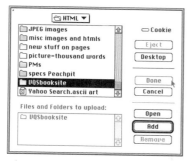

Figure 10-19. *Select each folder or file that you wish to transfer to the server and click Add. When you've finished choosing folders and files, click Done.*

Figure 10-20. *Choose the Text format for Text files and the Raw Data format for Other Files.*

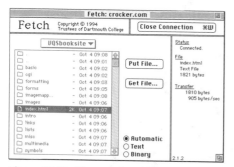

Figure 10-21. *The transferred files maintain the same hierarchy that they had on the Mac. Click Close Connection to close the connection to the server.*

7. Make sure the correct directory where you wish to place your set of HTML files is showing in the main Fetch window **(Figure 10-17)**.

8. Choose Put Folders and Files in the Remote menu **(Figure 10-18)**.

9. In the dialog box that appears, choose the files that you wish to transfer to the server and click Add. The files will appear at the bottom of the dialog box. When you have selected all the files you wish to transfer, click Done **(Figure 10-19)**.

10. In the Choose formats dialog box that appears, select the appropriate formats for the files. Use Text for HTML and other text documents and Raw Data for other kinds of files **(Figure 10-20)**.

11. Click OK. The files will be transferred to the server and will maintain the hierarchy that they had on the local system **(Figure 10-21)**. If folders already exist with the same names as those that you are transferring, the folders on the servers will be used (and their contents preserved, unless the files transferred also have the same names).

12. Click Close Connection to close the connection to the server.

✔ **Tip**

■ If you have used relative URLs (see page 3), these will be maintained when you transfer the entire folder or directory from your computer to the server. If you have used absolute URLs, you will have to change them to reflect the files' new locations.

Transferring files (Mac)

To transfer files to the server with WS_FTP:

1. Open WS_FTP.

2. In the Session Profile dialog box that appears **(Figure 10-22)**, click New to create a new set of preferences (or select an existing profile if you've already created it.)

3. Give the profile a name in the Profile Name box.

4. Enter the Host name of the server, the Host type (Automatic detect, if you're not sure), your User ID and Password.

5. Enter the desired directory on the server where you plan to transfer the files in the Remote Host area at the bottom of the dialog box. If you like, you can also enter the directory on the local PC from which you will transfer the files.

6. Click Save to save the profile.

7. Click OK to open the connection.

8. Click Options at the bottom of the WS_FTP window **(Figure 10-23)**.

9. Click the Extensions button **(Figure 10-24)**.

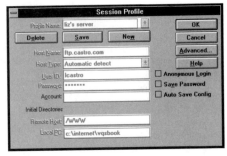

Figure 10-22. *After clicking New in WS_FTP, enter the information necessary for connecting to the server, including the server's name (Host Name), the Host type, your user ID and password.*

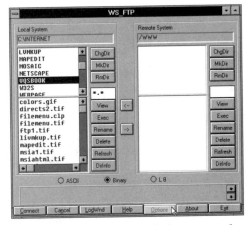

Figure 10-23. *Click Options at the bottom part of the main WS_FTP window.*

Figure 10-24. *Click the Extensions button in the Options dialog box.*

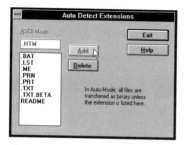

Figure 10-25. *Type .htm in the text box and then click Add so that the HTML documents will be transferred in ASCII format, even with Binary format selected in the main window.*

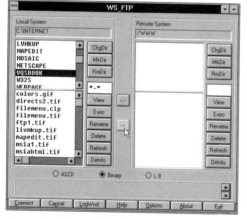

Figure 10-26. *Select the desired directory (or directories) and then click the right pointing arrow in the middle of the dialog box.*

10. Type .htm in the text box and click Add so that your HTML documents will be transferred in ASCII format **(Figure 10-25)**.

11. Click Exit in both dialog boxes to return to the main window.

12. Make sure the Binary option is selected at the bottom of the main window. This applies to all files with extensions not appearing in the Auto Detect Extensions dialog box.

13. Choose the files that you wish to transfer from the left side of the window by clicking on them. You may have to create directories on the server with the MkDir button.

14. Click the right pointing arrow to begin the transfer **(Figure 10-26)**.

15. Repeat steps 13-14 as needed.

16. Close the connection to the server.

Changing permissions

Whether you transfer the files from a Mac or PC, or even another UNIX machine, if your server is a UNIX machine, you will have to change the permissions of the transferred files to open access to your pages to the public. However, you may not have the necessary privileges to change the permissions. In that case, contact your server administrator.

Figure 10-27. *After opening the connection with the File menu, log in by typing your user name and password.*

To change permissions:

1. Open a Telnet program, like NCSA Telnet for Mac or Ewan for Windows.

2. Enter the server name in the Host box and click Connect. You will be connected to the server as if you were at a local terminal.

3. Log in with your User ID and Password. Generally, you will find yourself automatically in your personal directory on the server. **(Figure 10-27)**.

4. If necessary, type **cd directory** where *directory* is the desired directory you wish to view **(Figure 10-28)**. Type **ls** to list the directory's contents.

Figure 10-28. *Use the cd command to go to the directory that contains the files or directories whose permissions you wish to change.*

5. Type **chmod o+rx name** where *name* is the name of the directory or file whose permissions will be changed **(Figure 10-29)**.

6. Type **lo** to log out.

✔ Tips

■ Type **man chmod** for more information about the chmod command.

■ HTML files and images need *read-only* permission (the *r* in o+rx); CGI scripts need *execute* permission (the *x* in o+rx).

Figure 10-29. *Type chmod o+rx followed by the name of the file or directory whose permissions you wish to change.*

Figure 10-30. *Both Netscape (left) and Mosaic include menu commands for jumping to their respective What's New services.*

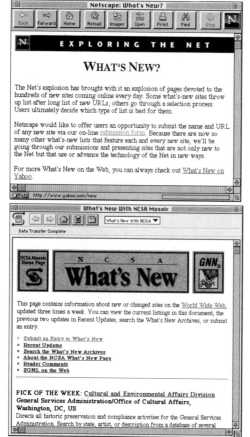

Figure 10-31. *What's New pages (Netscape above, NCSA Mosaic below) give links to recently created pages and allow designers (like you) to submit information about their new pages.*

Advertising your site

Before you start talking up your site in public, you should test it once again (see pages 138-139) and make sure that everything works as it should. Once you are satisfied you can begin to recruit users.

To advertise your site:

1. Use the What's New fill in forms at free Web indexing services like Yahoo, Netscape and Mosaic **(Figure 10-30 and 10-31)**. You can either use the menu commands available in individual programs, or type the URL:

Yahoo: *http://www.yahoo.com/bin/menu1?247,18*

Netscape: *http://home.netscape.com/home/whats-new.html*

Mosaic: *http://www.ncsa.uiuc.edu/SDG/Software/Mosaic/Docs/whats-new.html*

(There are no spaces in any of these URLs. The hyphens are *not* optional.)

2. Pay a company to advertise your page for you.

3. Post a note in the moderated UseNet newsgroup *comp.infosystems.www. announce* or the unmoderated *comp.internet.net-happenings* or in newsgroups that have similar interests as your Web site.

4. Send e-mail to your associates and friends. (You can include the URL for your site in all your correspondence in a signature.)

5. Send e-mail to the creators of other sites with similar interests or topics.

Advertising your site

HTML TOOLS

HTML Editors

You can use *any* text editor to write HTML, including SimpleText or TeachText on the Macintosh, Write for Windows, or vi in Unix systems. The HTML code produced with these simpler programs is no different from the HTML produced by more complex HTML editors.

A simple text editor is like the most basic SLR 35 mm camera. You have to set your f-stop and aperture manually, and then focus before shooting. The dedicated HTML editors are point-and-shoot cameras: just aim and fire, for a price. They are more expensive, and generally less flexible.

HTML editors

What HTML editors offer

Dedicated HTML editors offer the following advantages over simple text editors (of course, not every HTML editor has every feature):

- they insert opening and closing tags with a single click

- they check and verify syntax in your HTML and typos in your text

- they allow you to add attributes by clicking buttons instead of typing words in a certain order in a certain place in the document

- they offer varying degrees of WYSIWYG display of your Web page

- they correct mistakes in existing HTML pages

- they simplify the use of special characters

Disadvantages of HTML editors

These extra features come at a price, however. Some things that may annoy you about HTML editors is that

- they don't all recognize new or nonstandard HTML codes (like Netscape extensions)

- they don't all support forms and tables

- they are more difficult to learn, and less intuitive than they promise

- they are expensive (all simple text editors are included free with the respective system software)

- they use up more space on disk and more memory

- they add proprietary information (like their name, for example) to the HTML document

HTML editors

Figure 11-1. *HoTMetaL's unique way to show HTML tags as icons means you can't misspell or mistype them, and they stand out clearly from the contents of the page.*

Figure 11-2. *Choose Hide Tags in HoTMetaL Pro's View menu to see the HTML document without tags.*

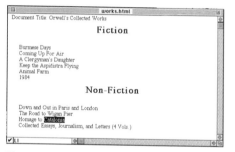

Figure 11-3. *Looking at the page without tags gives you a better idea of what your users will see.*

HoTMetaL Pro

HoTMetaL Pro is the successful HTML editor from SoftQuad, one of the pioneers in the HTML editing field. Although earlier versions of HoTMetaL were a bit neurotic about a misplaced angle bracket in imported HTML text, version 2 accepts HTML 3 and Netscape extensions (albeit with a warning) and quietly corrects minor errors in imported documents.

HoTMetaL includes a powerful spell checker and thesaurus to make sure the contents of your Web page are as polished as possible. When you type a special character like ñ, HoTMetaL automatically converts the character into its character entity.

Possibly one of HoTMetaL's most important features is its ability to check a document for proper HTML syntax. You can check documents you've created with HoTMetaL, or import other documents and check them. Once validated in this way, you can be sure that they will be viewed correctly by the browser (as long as you haven't used nonstandard HTML tags).

The Windows and Unix versions of HoTMetaL let you import text in Microsoft Word and WordPerfect format and converts them to HTML code (as much as is possible).

Finally, HoTMetaL offers a shortcut command to access a browser so that you can preview your page and adjust it as necessary.

HoTMetaL (SoftQuad, $200) takes up a hefty 5 Mb of hard disk and requires at least 3.5 Mb of RAM. It could be a lot faster.

HTML editors

BBEdit HTML Tools

BBEdit, from Bare Bones Software, is a powerful little text editor. There is a free, very bare edition (version 1.5) and a complete version that retails for $120. Either version of the principal program works just fine with the two principal sets of additions for HTML: BBEdit HTML Tools and BBEdit HTML Extensions.

Both collections contain a set of freeware add-ons to BBEdit that help you insert tags for anchors, links, images, paragraphs, headers and the like. You can find BBEdit HTML Extensions, by Carles Bellver, at *http://www.uji.es/bbedit-html-extensions.html*. Lindsay Davies' HTML Tools can be found at *http://www.york.ac.uk/~ld11/BBEditTools.html*.

Generally, to write HTML with BBEdit and the extensions (or tools), you first choose the text to format and then double click the appropriate extension. The corresponding tags are inserted before (and after, if necessary) the selected text.

Figure 11-4. *The BBEdit tools appear in a separate menu. Select text and then choose a tool to apply it.*

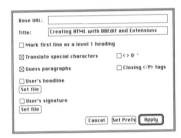

Figure 11-5. *If necessary, a dialog box will appear in which you can mark other options.*

HTML editors

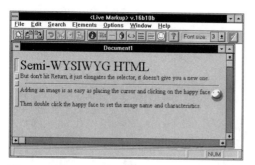

Figure 11-6. *Live Markup gives an almost WYSIWYG display of your HTML document as you create it. Unfortunately, its interface is less than standard.*

Live Markup (for Windows)

Once you figure out how to deal with the Live Markup's peculiarities, the program is a big help in creating HTML. Instead of fussing with opening and closing tags, Live Markup lets you browse your page as you create it in a semi-WYSIWYG environment.

Instead of showing tags, you see *selectors* in the left hand margin of the document. Every time the HTML code changes, a new selector appears; if the text continues without a change in HTML, the selector is elongated. Click on the selector to change certain attributes of the text.

To apply character-based formatting, select the desired text and click with the right mouse button. Then, choose the appropriate format from the pop-up menu that appears.

Live Markup strays too far from standard Windows commands, making the program less than intuitive. For example, you can't backspace beyond a selector; the cursor just stops. (Click with the right mouse button and select from the pop-up menu to delete.) You can't use the arrow keys to move from selector to selector (like from a Header to the paragraph that follows it), you have to use the mouse.

Despite its limitations, however, Live Markup can still be an aid to beginning Web designers who don't want to hassle with angle brackets and backslashes.

HTML editors

Microsoft Internet Assistant

Microsoft Internet Assistant is actually a add-on module for Word for Windows. After installing the module, you will be able to create new documents with the HTML or WebBrowse template, and save them in HTML format.

Once you have learned Word, Internet Assistant is easy to figure out. Perhaps the most important benefit of having Internet Assistant inside Word is that you can take advantage of many of Word's features, such as Spell Check, Auto Correct and even Styles.

To apply an HTML tag to text, simply choose the desired formatting from the menus. For example, to create a header, choose Styles in the Format menu and then Header 1, H1 in the dialog box.

To see what the page will look like once it is published, choose Web Browse. To view the HTML tags, you must save and close the document and then open it with the Confirm Conversions box checked in the Open dialog box. Click Text only in the dialog box that appears, and you'll be able to see the HTML tags.

There are two versions of Internet Assistant: one for Windows 95 and one for Windows 3.1. Both require specific versions of Microsoft Word. (For example, the Windows version requires version 6.0a or 6.0c of Microsoft Word. You can get a free update patch for version 6.0 at ftp://ftp.microsoft.com/Softlib/MSLFILES/WORD60A.EXE.)

Finally, a word of caution. Like all Microsoft Windows products, this one took me several hours to install, reinstall and make work (including one particularly fun reinstallation of Word itself). Once up, it's OK, if you make it.

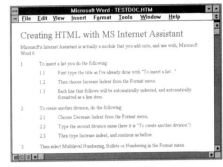

Figure 11-7. *The Microsoft Internet Assistant is a set of templates that are superimposed on the main Microsoft Word program. It has its own menus and commands.*

Figure 11-8. *View your HTML document by saving your document, closing it, and then reopening it as text.*

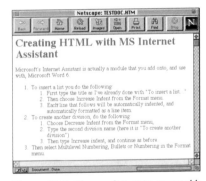

Figure 11-9. *The result is quite acceptable, as shown with Netscape.*

HTML editors

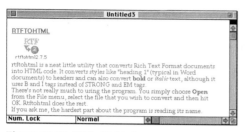

Figure 11-10. *With rtftohtml, you create your document as usual, applying character formatting to text and heading styles to your headers.*

Figure 11-11. *Save the document in RTF format.*

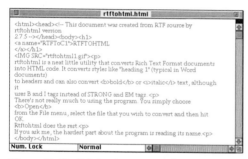

Figure 11-12. *Rtftohtml automatically converts heading styles and text formatting into proper HTML.*

Figure 11-13. *The converted document looks exactly as it should in Netscape, without typing a single angle bracket.*

HTML Filters

If you have existing documents that you want to convert into HTML, you will need an HTML filter that reads your document and uses as much information as it can to create the corresponding HTML tags. Some filters are very simple and can work with generic formats like Text only or RTF. Other filters are specifically designed for high-end page layout software like FrameMaker, PageMaker and QuarkXPress.

RTF to HTML

The unpronounceable rtftohtml (latest version 2.7.5) is an excellent utility for converting RTF format files into HTML pages. Most major word processors and page layout programs can export text in Rich Text Format (RTF), originally developed by Microsoft, maintaining character and paragraph formatting.

Rtftohtml can convert heading styles into HTML headers, bold and italic text into B and I tagged text and images into IMG references. But its most powerful feature is certainly its ability to take easily constructed tables in Word and convert them into beautiful tables in HTML.

To take full advantage of rtftohtml, you have to use styles in the original document, be it in Microsoft Word, PageMaker or whatever. Further, the styles used must either correspond to the default styles recognized by rtftohtml, or the relationship desired must be entered manually into the preferences file *html-trans*.

Rtftohtml is available for Macintosh, Unix, Sun, OS2 and DOS. It is freeware from Chris Hector. You can find it at *ftp:// ftp.cray.com/src/WWWstuff/RTF/latest/*

HTML filters

Text to HTML

This little program is simple and excellent. It converts text and RTF format documents into HTML code, while automatically adding graphics and creating an index.

To use Text to HTML, create a text document for each page on your Web site. Organize the documents in folders according to the hierarchy that they should have on your Web site. Then drag the entire main folder onto the Text to HTML icon, and select a destination folder for the resulting HTML documents, including the index.

To include graphics in your Web pages, place .gif or .jpg files with the same name as the corresponding Web page text document in the destination folder. The graphic will be placed directly after the first header by default; other options are available. Several types of images can be inserted automatically—name an image *bullet.gif* and it will be placed before every link to another converted document.

The resulting HTML code is simplicity itself. The first line is used both as TITLE and as H1 and the rest of the text is considered body text. Single returns are converted to BR and multiple returns are changed to P. Even if you need more complex documents, you can still use these as a starting point.

You can also use Text to HTML to create indexes for your site. Any HTML code that the program encounters remains intact. The only minor drawback is that each file's name is changed—although this is completely transparent to the user.

Figure 11-14. *One of the original text files.*

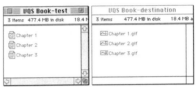

Figure 11-15. *Page files go in one folder while the corresponding images go in the destination folder.*

Figure 11-16. *After dragging the VQS book-test folder onto the TexttoHtml icon, the index and new HTML files are created in the destination folder.*

Figure 11-17. *TexttoHtml links the image to the text document and converts the whole thing to HTML.*

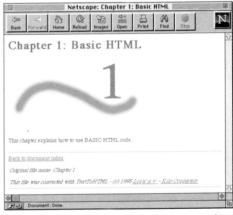

Figure 11-18. *TexttoHTML links the corresponding images to each file and then links the files themselves together and creates an index.*

HTML filters

Image map tools

As explained on pages 72-75, an image map is nothing more than a set of coordinates that show the position of a particular shape, along with the URL that the reader will jump to when they click in that shape. You can create an image map with a paper and pencil (and any graphics program that shows x and y coordinates) or you can use one of the following to speed up the process.

Both programs save in CERN or NCSA formats. Be sure and select the format that corresponds to your server.

Mapedit (for Windows and Unix)

This little utility from Thomas Boutell ($25, shareware) lets you open up a GIF file, use the mouse to outline the clickable areas of the image and then assign each area its corresponding URL. It is a bit of a no-frills program. Although it works correctly, and even has an excellent Help file, it's a little coarse.

For example, at first it seems obvious that you should select a shape from the Tools menu and then drag out the shape. In fact, the shape won't appear until you click the *right* mouse button—something more experienced Windows users might expect, but I doubt it.

Further, once you have created a shape, you cannot edit it. This is almost acceptable for rectangles, but try to trace a circle properly on your first try. If it's not right, you'll have to delete it (use Test/ Edit and then the Delete button in the dialog box that appears when you click on the offending area) and start over.

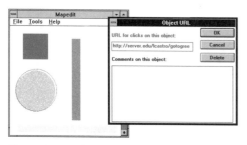

Figure 11-19. *Thomas Boutell's Mapedit is a bit rough around the edges, but it creates NCSA HTTPd and CERN server image maps just fine.*

Image map tools

WebMap (for Macintosh)

Mac users have a much more satisfying alternative. WebMap, from City.Net Express (http://www.city.net/cnx/software) has an immediately recognizable interface. You click on a shape, draw the shape, and then add the corresponding URL in the dialog box that appears.

If the shape isn't exactly what you had in mind, use the pointer tool to change the shape itself, or to move it around the image.

WebMap also provides a list so that you can check over your clickable areas and URLs before generating the final document.

Miscellaneous tools

Some tools defy categorization, but are still worth talking about. A great source of HTML authoring tools is Jon Wiederspan's page at http://www.uwtc.washington.edu/Computing/WWW/Mac/HTMLEdit.html.

URL Key

This little control panel for Macintosh lets you copy a URL from any program on the Mac that recognizes the clipboard (which is virtually all of them) and load it into your pre-specified browser.

It's a great shortcut and I'm glad they thought of it. If you need to convince yourself of its usefulness, download it, use it for a few days and then open the Control panel. It keeps track of how much you use it **(Figure 11-22)**.

URL Key is *pointerware*. If you like it and use it, the authors request that you add a link on your Web page to theirs.

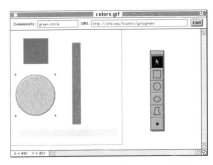

Figure 11-20. *WebMap for Macintosh is a simple, complete program for creating image maps.*

Figure 11-21. *You can list the areas already defined in WebMap so that you can edit or delete them.*

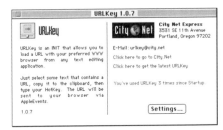

Figure 11-22. *Justify URL Key's usefulness by checking the stats in the main control panel window. Click Settings to choose your browser and hot key.*

SPECIAL SYMBOLS

You can type any letter of the English alphabet or any number into your HTML document and be confident that every other computer system will interpret it correctly. However, if your Web page contains any accents, foreign characters or special symbols, you may have to use a special code to make sure they appear correctly on the page.

The ISO Latin-1 character set is the standard for the World Wide Web. It assigns a number to each character, number or symbol in the set. In addition, some characters, especially the accented letters, have special names.

However, some computer systems, especially Macintosh and DOS, do not use the standard character set. That means that you could type a *é* in your HTML document and have it appear as a | (a straight vertical line) on your Web page.

To make sure accented characters and special characters appear correctly, no matter what system you write on, use the steps described on page 158 to enter them into your HTML document.

Using special symbols

The symbols numbered 32 to 126—which include all the letters in the English alphabet, the numbers and many common symbols—can be typed directly from the keyboard of any system. The symbols numbered 127 to 255 should be entered as described below.

To use special symbols:

1. Place the cursor where you wish the special character to appear.

2. Type **&**.

3. *Either* type **#n** where *n* is the number that corresponds to the desired symbol *or* type **name** where *name* is the code that corresponds to the desired symbol. (See the tables on pages 159-162.)

4. Type **;**.

5. Continue with your HTML document.

✔ **Tips**

■ All characters have a corresponding number. Not all characters have a corresponding name. It doesn't matter which one you use.

■ Netscape 1.1 doesn't recognize *í* code. To insert a small *í*, use the number *í*.

■ The character names are case sensitive. Type them exactly as they appear in the tables.

■ Although this system is supposed to eliminate differences across platforms, the tables illustrate that it is not 100% effective.

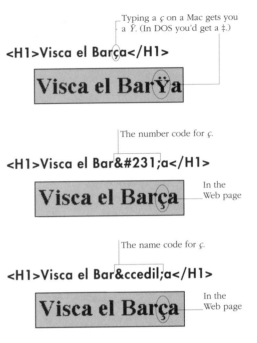

Typing a ç on a Mac gets you a Ÿ. (In DOS you'd get a ‡.)

`<H1>Visca el Barça</H1>`

The number code for ç.

`<H1>Visca el Bar&#231;a</H1>`

In the Web page

The name code for ç.

`<H1>Visca el Bar&ccedil;a</H1>`

In the Web page

Figure A-1. *To display a ç properly, you must use either its number or name. It looks awful in your HTML document, but on the Web page, where it counts, it's beautiful.*

On the Macintosh

Use the quote, ampersand, greater than sign and less than sign codes when you want to show actual HTML code on your page.

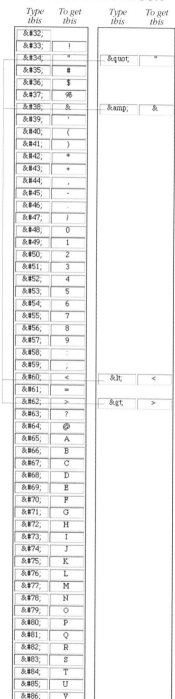

Type this	To get this	Type this	To get this
&#32;			
&#33;	!		
&#34;	"	&quot;	"
&#35;	#		
&#36;	$		
&#37;	%		
&#38;	&	&amp;	&
&#39;	'		
&#40;	(		
&#41;	)		
&#42;	*		
&#43;	+		
&#44;	,		
&#45;	-		
&#46;	.		
&#47;	/		
&#48;	0		
&#49;	1		
&#50;	2		
&#51;	3		
&#52;	4		
&#53;	5		
&#54;	6		
&#55;	7		
&#56;	8		
&#57;	9		
&#58;	:		
&#59;	;		
&#60;	<	&lt;	<
&#61;	=		
&#62;	>	&gt;	>
&#63;	?		
&#64;	@		
&#65;	A		
&#66;	B		
&#67;	C		
&#68;	D		
&#69;	E		
&#70;	F		
&#71;	G		
&#72;	H		
&#73;	I		
&#74;	J		
&#75;	K		
&#76;	L		
&#77;	M		
&#78;	N		
&#79;	O		
&#80;	P		
&#81;	Q		
&#82;	R		
&#83;	S		
&#84;	T		
&#85;	U		
&#86;	V		

On Windows

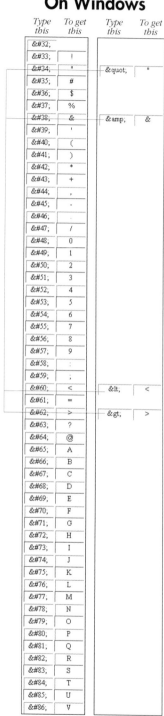

Type this	To get this	Type this	To get this
&#32;			
&#33;	!		
&#34;	"	&quot;	"
&#35;	#		
&#36;	$		
&#37;	%		
&#38;	&	&amp;	&
&#39;	'		
&#40;	(		
&#41;	)		
&#42;	*		
&#43;	+		
&#44;	,		
&#45;	-		
&#46;	.		
&#47;	/		
&#48;	0		
&#49;	1		
&#50;	2		
&#51;	3		
&#52;	4		
&#53;	5		
&#54;	6		
&#55;	7		
&#56;	8		
&#57;	9		
&#58;	:		
&#59;	;		
&#60;	<	&lt;	<
&#61;	=		
&#62;	>	&gt;	>
&#63;	?		
&#64;	@		
&#65;	A		
&#66;	B		
&#67;	C		
&#68;	D		
&#69;	E		
&#70;	F		
&#71;	G		
&#72;	H		
&#73;	I		
&#74;	J		
&#75;	K		
&#76;	L		
&#77;	M		
&#78;	N		
&#79;	O		
&#80;	P		
&#81;	Q		
&#82;	R		
&#83;	S		
&#84;	T		
&#85;	U		
&#86;	V		

Special symbols

On the Macintosh

Type this	To get this
W	W
X	X
Y	Y
Z	Z
[	[
\	\
]	]
^	^
_	_
`	`
a	a
b	b
c	c
d	d
e	e
f	f
g	g
h	h
i	i
j	j
k	k
l	l
m	m
n	n
o	o
p	p
q	q
r	r
s	s
t	t
u	u
v	v
w	w
x	x
y	y
z	z
{	{
|		
}	}
~	~
&#127;	]
€	▪
	™
‚	‚
ƒ	ƒ
„	„
…	…
†	
‡	‡
ˆ	^
‰	‰
Š	…
‹	‹
Œ	Œ
	Ÿ

There are no name codes for symbols 87 to 141. Use the number codes at left.

On Windows

Type this	To get this
W	W
X	X
Y	Y
Z	Z
[	[
\	\
]	]
^	^
_	_
`	`
a	a
b	b
c	c
d	d
e	e
f	f
g	g
h	h
i	i
j	j
k	k
l	l
m	m
n	n
o	o
p	p
q	q
r	r
s	s
t	t
u	u
v	v
w	w
x	x
y	y
z	z
{	{
|		
}	}
~	~
&#127;	▯
€	▯
	▯
‚	‚
ƒ	ƒ
„	„
…	…
†	†
‡	‡
ˆ	^
‰	‰
Š	Š
‹	‹
Œ	Œ
	▯

There are no name codes for symbols 87 to 141. Use the number codes at left.

Theoretically, characters 128-160 are nonprintable. As you can see, however, they do show up on Macs and Windows based computers.

Special symbols

On the Macintosh

Type this	To get this	Type this	To get this
&#142;	ı		
&#143;	∂		
&#143;	∂		
&#144;	Δ		
&#145;	'		
&#146;	'		
&#147;	"		
&#148;	"		
&#149;	•		
&#150;	–		
&#151;	—		
&#152;	˜		
&#153;	™		
&#154;	°		
&#155;	›		
&#156;	œ		
&#157;	ˇ		
&#158;	ı		
&#159;	Ÿ		
&#161;	¡		
&#162;	¢		
&#163;	£		
&#164;	¤		
&#165;	¥		
&#166;	¦		
&#167;	§		
&#168;	¨		
&#169;	©		
&#170;	ª		
&#171;	«		
&#172;	¬		
&#173;	-		
&#174;	®		
&#175;	¯		
&#176;	°		
&#177;	±		
&#178;	2		
&#179;	3		
&#180;	´		
&#181;	µ		
&#182;	¶		
&#183;	·		
&#184;	¸		
&#185;	1		
&#186;	º		
&#187;	»		
&#188;	π		
&#189;	∏		
&#190;	≤		
&#191;	¿		
&#192;	À	&Agrave;	À
&#193;	Á	&Aacute;	Á
&#194;	Â	&Acirc;	Â
&#195;	Ã	&Atilde;	Ã
&#196;	Ä	&Auml;	Ä

On Windows

Type this	To get this	Type this	To get this
&#142;	□		
&#143;	□		
&#143;	□		
&#144;	□		
&#145;	'		
&#146;	'		
&#147;	"		
&#148;	"		
&#149;	•		
&#150;	–		
&#151;	—		
&#152;	˜		
&#153;	™		
&#154;	š		
&#155;	›		
&#156;	œ		
&#157;	□		
&#158;	□		
&#159;	Ÿ		
&#161;	¡		
&#162;	¢		
&#163;	£		
&#164;	¤		
&#165;	¥		
&#166;	¦		
&#167;	§		
&#168;	¨		
&#169;	©		
&#170;	ª		
&#171;	«		
&#172;	¬		
&#173;	-		
&#174;	®		
&#175;	¯		
&#176;	°		
&#177;	±		
&#178;	2		
&#179;	1		
&#180;	´		
&#181;	µ		
&#182;	¶		
&#183;			
&#184;	¸		
&#185;	1		
&#186;	º		
&#187;	»		
&#188;	¼		
&#189;	½		
&#190;	¾		
&#191;	¿		
&#192;	À	&Agrave;	À
&#193;	Á	&Aacute;	Á
&#194;	Â	&Acirc;	Â
&#195;	Ã	&Atilde;	Ã
&#196;	Ä	&Auml;	Ä

Symbols 188 to 190 are the first to show clear differences on Mac and Windows based machines.

Special symbols

On the Macintosh

Type this	To get this	Type this	To get this
&#197;	Å	&Aring;	Å
&#198;	Æ	&AElig;	Æ
&#199;	Ç	&Ccedil;	Ç
&#200;	È	&Egrave;	È
&#201;	É	&Eacute;	É
&#202;	Ê	&Ecirc;	Ê
&#203;	Ë	&Euml;	Ë
&#204;	Ì	&Igrave;	Ì
&#205;	Í	&Iacute;	Í
&#206;	Î	&Icirc;	Î
&#207;	Ï	&Iuml;	Ï
&#208;	‹	&ETH;	‹
&#209;	Ñ	&Ntilde;	Ñ
&#210;	Ò	&Ograve;	Ò
&#211;	Ó	&Oacute;	Ó
&#212;	Ô	&Ocirc;	Ô
&#213;	Õ	&Otilde;	Õ
&#214;	Ö	&Ouml;	Ö
&#215;	x		
&#216;	Ø	&Oslash;	Ø
&#217;	Ù	&Ugrave;	Ù
&#218;	Ú	&Uacute;	Ú
&#219;	Û	&Ucirc;	Û
&#220;	Ü	&Uuml;	Ü
&#221;		&Yacute;	
&#222;	ñ	&THORN;	ñ
&#223;	ß	&szlig;	ß
&#224;	à	&agrave;	à
&#225;	á	&aacute;	á
&#226;	â	&acirc;	â
&#227;	ã	&atilde;	ã
&#228;	ä	&auml;	ä
&#229;	å	&aring;	å
&#230;	æ	&aelig;	æ
&#231;	ç	&ccedil;	ç
&#232;	è	&egrave;	è
&#233;	é	&eacute;	é
&#234;	ê	&ecirc;	ê
&#235;	ë	&euml;	ë
&#236;	ì	&igrave;	ì
&#237;	í	&iacute;	í
&#238;	î	&icirc;	î
&#239;	ï	&iuml;	ï
&#240;	›	&eth;	›
&#241;	ñ	&ntilde;	ñ
&#242;	ò	&ograve;	ò
&#243;	ó	&oacute;	ó
&#244;	ô	&ocirc;	ô
&#245;	õ	&otilde;	õ
&#246;	ö	&ouml;	ö
&#247;	÷		
&#248;	ø	&oslash;	ø
&#249;	ù	&ugrave;	ù
&#250;	ú	&uacute;	ú
&#251;	û	&ucirc;	û
&#252;	ü	&uuml;	ü
&#253;	‡	&yacute;	‡
&#254;	fl	&thorn;	fl
&#255;	ÿ	&yuml;	ÿ

The Eth (a character used in Old English and Modern Icelandic) is not available on the Mac.

Also missing from the Mac are the Y with an acute accent and the Thorn (another Icelandic letter)—both capital and small forms.

No small eth.

No small Y with acute accent nor small thorn.

On Windows

Type this	To get this	Type this	To get this
&#197;	Å	&Aring;	Å
&#198;	Æ	&AElig;	Æ
&#199;	Ç	&Ccedil;	Ç
&#200;	È	&Egrave;	È
&#201;	É	&Eacute;	É
&#202;	Ê	&Ecirc;	Ê
&#203;	Ë	&Euml;	Ë
&#204;	Ì	&Igrave;	Ì
&#205;	Í	&Iacute;	Í
&#206;	Î	&Icirc;	Î
&#207;	Ï	&Iuml;	Ï
&#208;	Ð	&ETH;	Ð
&#209;	Ñ	&Ntilde;	Ñ
&#210;	Ò	&Ograve;	Ò
&#211;	Ó	&Oacute;	Ó
&#212;	Ô	&Ocirc;	Ô
&#213;	Õ	&Otilde;	Õ
&#214;	Ö	&Ouml;	Ö
&#215;	×		
&#216;	Ø	&Oslash;	Ø
&#217;	Ù	&Ugrave;	Ù
&#218;	Ú	&Uacute;	Ú
&#219;	Û	&Ucirc;	Û
&#220;	Ü	&Uuml;	Ü
&#221;	Ý	&Yacute;	Ý
&#222;	Þ	&THORN;	Þ
&#223;	ß	&szlig;	ß
&#224;	à	&agrave;	à
&#225;	á	&aacute;	á
&#226;	â	&acirc;	â
&#227;	ã	&atilde;	ã
&#228;	ä	&auml;	ä
&#229;	å	&aring;	å
&#230;	æ	&aelig;	æ
&#231;	ç	&ccedil;	ç
&#232;	è	&egrave;	è
&#233;	é	&eacute;	é
&#234;	ê	&ecirc;	ê
&#235;	ë	&euml;	ë
&#236;	ì	&igrave;	ì
&#237;	í	&iacute;	í
&#238;	î	&icirc;	î
&#239;	ï	&iuml;	ï
&#240;	ð	&eth;	ð
&#241;	ñ	&ntilde;	ñ
&#242;	ò	&ograve;	ò
&#243;	ó	&oacute;	ó
&#244;	ô	&ocirc;	ô
&#245;	õ	&otilde;	õ
&#246;	ö	&ouml;	ö
&#247;	÷		
&#248;	ø	&oslash;	ø
&#249;	ù	&ugrave;	ù
&#250;	ú	&uacute;	ú
&#251;	û	&ucirc;	û
&#252;	ü	&uuml;	ü
&#253;	ý	&yacute;	ý
&#254;	þ	&thorn;	þ
&#255;	ÿ	&yuml;	ÿ

COLORS IN HEX

With Netscape's extensions, you can choose the color for the background of your page as well as for the text and links. Instead of using subjective terms like *light blue* or *sienna*, you specify the color by giving its red, green and blue components—in the form of a number between 0 and 255. To make things really complicated, you must specify these components with the hexadecimal equivalent of that number. The table on page 165 gives the corresponding hexadecimal number for each possible value of red, green or blue.

Check the inside back cover for a full-color table of many common colors, together with their hexadecimal codes.

Finding a color's RGB components—in hex

The inside back cover contains a full-color table of many common colors and their hexadecimal equivalents. If you don't see the color you want, you can use Photoshop (or other image editing program) to display the red, green and blue components of the colors you want to use on your page. Then consult the table on page 165 for the hexadecimal equivalents of those components.

To find a color's RGB components:

1. In Photoshop, click one of the color boxes in the tool box **(Figure B-1)**.

2. In the Color picker dialog box that appears, choose the desired color.

3. Write down the numbers that appear in the R, G and B text boxes. These numbers represent the R, G and B components of the color **(Fig. B-2)**.

4. Use the table on the next page to find the hexadecimal equivalents of the numbers found in step 3.

5. Assemble the hexadecimal numbers in the form *#rrggbb* where *rr* is the hexadecimal equivalent for the red component, *gg* is the hexadecimal equivalent for the green component and *bb* is the hexadecimal equivalent of the blue component.

✔ Tip

■ You can find instructions for specifying the background color on page 55, for specifying the text color on page 26 and for specifying the links' color on page 27.

Figure B-1. *In Photoshop, click on one of the color boxes in the toolbox to make the Color Picker dialog box appear.*

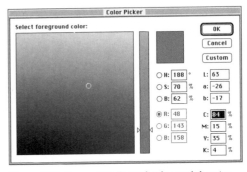

Figure B-2. *Choose the desired color and then jot down the values shown in the R, G and B text boxes. This color, a teal blue, has an R of 48 (hex=30), a G of 143 (hex=8F) and a B of 158 (hex =9E). Therefore, the hexadecimal equivalent of this color would be #308F9E.*

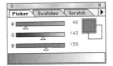

Figure B-3. *You can also use the Picker palette to choose colors and see their RGB components*

Finding a color's RGB components

Hexadecimal equivalents to the numbers 0-255

#	Hex	#	Hex	#	Hex	#	Hex	#	Hex	#	Hex	#	Hex	#	Hex
0	0	32	20	64	40	96	60	128	80	160	A0	192	C0	224	E0
1	1	33	21	65	41	97	61	129	81	161	A1	193	C1	225	E1
2	2	34	22	66	42	98	62	130	82	162	A2	194	C2	226	E2
3	3	35	23	67	43	99	63	131	83	163	A3	195	C3	227	E3
4	4	36	24	68	44	100	64	132	84	164	A4	196	C4	228	E4
5	5	37	25	69	45	101	65	133	85	165	A5	197	C5	229	E5
6	6	38	26	70	46	102	66	134	86	166	A6	198	C6	230	E6
7	7	39	27	71	47	103	67	135	87	167	A7	199	C7	231	E7
8	8	40	28	72	48	104	68	136	88	168	A8	200	C8	232	E8
9	9	41	29	73	49	105	69	137	89	169	A9	201	C9	233	E9
10	A	42	2A	74	4A	106	6A	138	8A	170	AA	202	CA	234	EA
11	B	43	2B	75	4B	107	6B	139	8B	171	AB	203	CB	235	EB
12	C	44	2C	76	4C	108	6C	140	8C	172	AC	204	CC	236	EC
13	D	45	2D	77	4D	109	6D	141	8D	173	AD	205	CD	237	ED
14	E	46	2E	78	4E	110	6E	142	8E	174	AE	206	CE	238	EE
15	F	47	2F	79	4F	111	6F	143	8F	175	AF	207	CF	239	EF
16	10	48	30	80	50	112	70	144	90	176	B0	208	D0	240	F0
17	11	49	31	81	51	113	71	145	91	177	B1	209	D1	241	F1
18	12	50	32	82	52	114	72	146	92	178	B2	210	D2	242	F2
19	13	51	33	83	53	115	73	147	93	179	B3	211	D3	243	F3
20	14	52	34	84	54	116	74	148	94	180	B4	212	D4	244	F4
21	15	53	35	85	55	117	75	149	95	181	B5	213	D5	245	F5
22	16	54	36	86	56	118	76	150	96	182	B6	214	D6	246	F6
23	17	55	37	87	57	119	77	151	97	183	B7	215	D7	247	F7
24	18	56	38	88	58	120	78	152	98	184	B8	216	D8	248	F8
25	19	57	39	89	59	121	79	153	99	185	B9	217	D9	249	F9
26	1A	58	3A	90	5A	122	7A	154	9A	186	BA	218	DA	250	FA
27	1B	59	3B	91	5B	123	7B	155	9B	187	BB	219	DB	251	FB
28	1C	60	3C	92	5C	124	7C	156	9C	188	BC	220	DC	252	FC
29	1D	61	3D	93	5D	125	7D	157	9D	189	BD	221	DD	253	FD
30	1E	62	3E	94	5E	126	7E	158	9E	190	BE	222	DE	254	FE
31	1F	63	3F	95	5F	127	7F	159	9F	191	BF	223	DF	255	FF

The Hexadecimal system

"Regular" numbers are based on the base 10 system, that is, there are ten symbols (what we call numbers): 0, 1, 2, 3, 4, 5, 6, 7, 8, and 9. To represent numbers greater than 9, we use a combination of these symbols where the first digit specifies how many *ones,* the second digit (to the left) specifies how many *tens* and so on.

In the hexadecimal system, which is base 16, there are sixteen symbols: 0, 1, 2, 3, 4, 5, 6, 7, 8, 9, a, b, c, d, e, and f. To represent numbers greater than *f* (which in base 10 we understand as *15*), we again use a combination of symbols. This time the first digit specifies how many ones, but the second digit (again, to the left) specifies how many sixteens. Thus, 10 is one *sixteen* and no *ones,* or simply *16* (as represented in base 10).

In addition to colors, you can use hexadecimal numbers to represent special symbols in URLs. Find the corresponding number in the table on pages 158-161, convert it to hexadecimal with the above table and precede it with a percent sign (%). Thus, the space, which is number 32, and has a hexadecimal equivalent of 20, can be represented as %20.

Hexadecimal equivalents

INDEX

Index

SUP tag 18
superscripts 18
symbols
    in file names 136
    in ordered lists 78
    special
        table 157
        use of 4

T

table of contents
    and anchors 64
TABLE tag 86–99
    BORDER attribute 89
    CELLPADDING attribute 91
    CELLSPACING attribute 91
    HEIGHT attribute 92
    WIDTH attribute 92
tables 85–98
    aligning cell's contents 96
    and forms 102
    and HTML editors 148
    and preformatted text 21
    borders 89
    captions 90
    cell spacing and padding 91
    creating in Microsoft Word 132
    headers across top 87
    headers along side 86
    headers on top and left 88
    mapping out 99
    simple 86
    spanning cells across columns 94
    spanning cells across rows 95
tags 1
    definition x
    in this book 1
    nesting 2
    order of 2
TD tag 86–99
    ALIGN attribute 96
    COLSPAN attribute 94
    HEIGHT attribute 93
    NOWRAP attribute 98
    ROWSPAN attribute 95
    VALIGN attribute 96
    WIDTH attribute 93
TeachText 1, 147
templates, creating 6
testing 138
    color combinations 28

text
    alternative 34. *See also* alternative text
    blinking 25
    block quotes 20
    blue 61
    bold (logical) 14
    bold (physical) 15
    centering 19
    clickable 61
    color 26
    emphasis 14
    font size 22–24
    formatting 14
    in monospaced fonts 16
    italics (logical) 14
    italics (physical) 15
    preformatted 21
    stopping wrap around images 51
    strike out 17
    subscripts 18
    superscripts 18
    underlined 61
    underlining 17
    wrapping around images 49–50
text areas. *See* text blocks
TEXT attribute, in BODY tag 26
text blocks 107
text boxes 103
text editors 147–154
Text to HTML (program) 154
TEXTAREA tag 107
    COLS attribute 107
    ROWS attribute 107
TH tag 86–99
    ALIGN attribute 96
    COLSPAN attribute 94
    HEIGHT attribute 93
    NOWRAP attribute 98
    ROWSPAN attribute 95
    VALIGN attribute 96
    WIDTH attribute 93
TIFF images 117
tiled images 57
TITLE tag 8
    and blinking text 25
    multiple 127
titles 8
    and formatting 14
    animated 127
    in tables 90
TR tag 86–99
transferring files to server 140
transparency 47
TT tag 16

POCKET

Index